The Best of *Sew News*:

SEW iT ALL

SEWING
MADE
SIMPLE

Quick Projects

WE ALL WISH sewing could be easier, faster and more fun, right? Well that's what *Sew it All* is all about! With the right tools at your fingertips, you'll find that sewing doesn't have to be difficult. You can take shortcuts without sacrificing quality (we promise!).

Turn the pages to find tons of projects that are simple enough for a beginner yet exciting enough for an expert. Whatever your skill level, you'll love the garments, accessories and home décor that are easily completed in no time.

Enjoy and have fun!

Find more free patterns and tutorials at sewitallmag.com and watch *Sew it All* episodes at sew.tv.

the art of everyday living

www.leisurearts.com

SEW iT ALL

741 Corporate Circle, Ste. A
Golden, CO, 80401
sewnews.com

SEW IT ALL STAFF
Editorial
Editor-in-Chief: Ellen March
Senior Editor: Beth Bradley
Associate Editor: Nicole LaFoille
Web Editor: Jill Case
Editorial Assistant: Jessica Giardino

Art
Creative Director: Sue Dothage
Graphic Designer: Erin Hershey
Assistant Graphic Designer: Courtney Kraig
Illustrator: Melinda Bylow
Photography: Bryce Boyer, Brent Ward, Mellisa Karlin Mahoney
Hair & Makeup Stylists: Angela Lewis

CREATIVE CRAFTS GROUP
SVP/General Manager: Tina Battock
SVP/Chief Marketing Officer: Nicole McGuire
VP/Production & Technology: Barbara Schmitz

OPERATIONS
Associate Publisher: Wendy Thompson
Circulation Manager: Deb Westmaas
New Business Manager: Adriana Maldonado
Renewal and Billing Manager: Nekeya Dancy
Digital Marketing Director: Kristen Allen
Digital Marketing Manager: Jodi Lee
Newsstand Consultant: TJ Montilli
Production Manager: Michael J. Rueckwald
Product and Video Development:
Kristi Loeffelholz
Advertising Coordinator: Madalene Becker
Administrative Assistant: Jane Flynn
Retail Sales: LaRita Godfrey: (800) 815-3538

F+W MEDIA INC.
Chairman & CEO: David Nussbaum
CFO & COO: James Ogle
President: Sara Domville
President: David Blansfield
Chief Digital Officer: Chad Phelps
VP/E-Commerce: Lucas Hilbert
Senior VP/Operations: Phil Graham
VP/Communications: Stacie Berger

LEISURE ARTS STAFF
Editorial Staff
Vice President of Editorial: Susan White Sullivan
Creative Art Director: Katherine Laughlin
Publications Director: Leah Lampirez
Special Projects Director: Susan Frantz Wiles
Prepress Technician: Stephanie Johnson

Business Staff
President and Chief Executive Officer:
Rick Barton
Senior Vice President of Operations:
Jim Dittrich
Vice President of Finance: Fred F. Pruss
Vice President of Sales-Retail Books:
Martha Adams
Vice President of Mass Market:
Bob Bewighouse
Vice President of Technology and Planning:
Laticia Mull Dittrich
Controller: Tiffany P. Childers
Information Technology Director: Brian Roden
Director of E-Commerce: Mark Hawkins
Manager of E-Commerce: Robert Young
Retail Customer Service Manager: Stan Raynor

Library of Congress Control Number: 2014934758
ISBN-13/EAN: 978-1-4647-1547-1
UPC: 0-28906-06315-8

CONTENTS

52

20

4

PUCKER UP

by Sue Barnabee

Make a pretty shirred scarf to coordinate with your fall wardrobe.

Check out **Sew it All episode 301**, "A Shirr Thing" for instructions to make a pretty shirred dress. Visit sewitalltv.com and sew.tv for more information.

Look to "Shirr Things" on page 6 for helpful shirring techniques and tips for using elastic thread.

SUPPLIES

3 yards of lightweight fabric (such as rayon challis)

Thread: elastic & matching all-purpose

Size 70/10 universal needle

Chalk marker

Tapestry needle

CUT IT

From the fabric, cut one rectangle measuring 12"x the fabric width.

SEW IT

Thread the machine with matching all-purpose thread in the needle and bobbin. Double-fold each rectangle long edge ¼" toward the wrong side; stitch.

Designate one rectangle short edge as the upper edge. Chalk-mark a line parallel to and 2" from the upper edge on the rectangle right side. Set the machine for a 1mm-wide and 3mm-long zigzag stitch; stitch along the line (1). Repeat to mark and stitch the rectangle lower edge.

Fold the rectangle in half lengthwise with right sides together; unfold. Chalk-mark the foldline, beginning and ending at the zigzag stitching. Chalk-mark a line parallel to and 1" from each rectangle long edge, beginning and ending at the zigzag stitching lines (2).

Hand-wind the elastic thread onto a bobbin. Don't wind the bobbin too tight, as the thread could break. Insert the bobbin into the machine, and then bring the thread up through the throatplate.

Set the machine for a 4mm-long straight stitch. Holding the rectangle taut, stitch the centerline slowly with the fabric right side facing up, beginning and ending the stitching ⅛" from the zigzag stitching and leaving long thread tails at the stitching beginning and end. Note: Don't fret if the fabric doesn't immediately gather after stitching the first row, as it typically gathers after stitching several rows.

Repeat to stitch ¼" from each side of the centerline, stretching the fabric along the previous stitched row as you sew. Stitch ¼" from each previous stitching row, creating five stitching rows.

Repeat to stitch five rows along the remaining drawn lines, creating three shirred sections (3). Steam-press each section to tightly gather the shirring.

Thread a tapestry needle with one thread tail. Weave the thread tail through several stitches on the scarf wrong side; knot the end. Repeat to weave and knot the remaining thread tails.

Fray the scarf ends by removing the crosswise threads up to each zigzag stitching line. ✪

SOURCE
Nancy's Notions carries elastic thread: (800) 833-0690, nancysnotions.com.

1.  ↕ 2"

2. 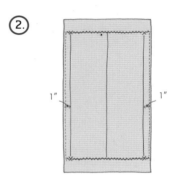 1"   1"

3.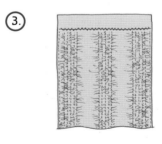

(TiP)

Test-stitch several rows on scrap fabric to determine if the stitching is satisfactory. If the elastic thread is too tight or loose on the fabric wrong side, reference the machine manual to adjust the tension accordingly.

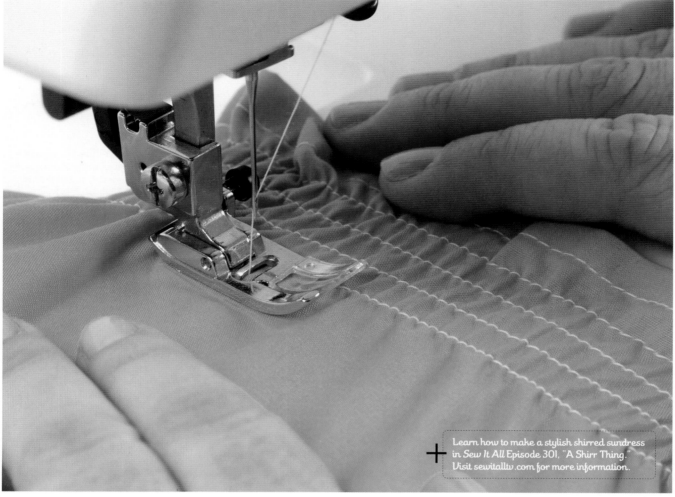

Learn how to make a stylish shirred sundress in *Sew It All* Episode 301, "A Shirr Thing." Visit sewitalltv.com for more information.

SHIRR THINGS

Shirring is a simple gathering technique that adds terrific texture to garments, accessories and home-dec projects. Learn how to easily shirr fabric and discover handy tools to simplify the process.

CHIC SHIRRING

Shirring can be decorative, functional or both, depending on its placement on a project. Shirring is composed of gathered stitching lines that draw the fabric inward, so the technique is often used to create shaping within a garment. The gathered stitching lines produce bulk, so the technique works best on light- to mediumweight fabrics. If shirring along an edge that requires a hem, finish the fabric raw edge first to neatly stitch the puckered fabric edge. The method used to shirr fabric depends on the project's end use.

STATIONARY SHIRRING

If the shirred area won't experience any stretching or stress, such as decorative shirring along a shoulder seam or curtain upper edge, create the shirred effect by using a gathering technique.

Mark the shirring lines on the fabric as desired or according to the pattern markings. The closer the stitching lines, the more tightly gathered the fabric will be.

Thread the machine with all-purpose thread in the needle and bobbin. Select a 3mm to 4mm stitch length.

Stitch along the first shirring line, leaving long thread tails (1). Repeat to stitch along each remaining shirring line (2).

Gently pull the bobbin thread tails of the first stitching line, evenly distributing the gathers as desired (3). Repeat to evenly gather the remaining stitching lines, and then pull the upper thread tails to the fabric wrong side (4).

Trim and knot the thread tails on the fabric wrong side (5). Lightly press the shirred area, using a steam iron.

As an alternative, use a specialty machine or serger shirring or gathering foot. Install the foot onto the machine, and then follow the foot manufacturer's instructions to shirr the fabric.

STRETCHY SHIRRING

If the shirred area requires stretching, such as a dress bodice, use elastic thread to shirr the fabric.

Mark the shirring lines on the fabric as desired or according to the pattern markings. Or use the presser foot right edge as a guide to evenly space the shirring lines. Align the presser foot edge with each previous shirring line during stitching.

Thread the machine needle with all-purpose thread. For a subtle effect, use matching thread. For a bolder look, use contrasting thread.

Wind a bobbin by hand with elastic thread, using a small amount of tension but making sure not to stretch the thread (6). Evenly distribute the thread on the bobbin. Don't attempt to wind elastic thread onto the bobbin using the machine, as the thread is too thick to pass through the machine thread guides. Install the bobbin into the machine and draw up the elastic thread through the throatplate hole.

Select a 3mm to 4mm stitch length. Test-stitch on a fabric scrap to determine

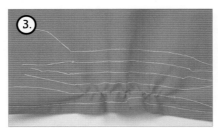

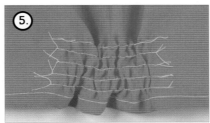

shirred effect. If needed, lower the upper tension and/or adjust the stitch length.

With the fabric right side facing up, stitch the first shirring line, backstitching at the beginning and end to secure the thread (7). Repeat to stitch each successive shirring line, gently smoothing the fabric as you stitch to avoid stitching over a pucker or fold (8).

Hold a steam iron a few inches above the shirred area and blast with steam to tightly gather the shirring. Lightly press the finished edge.

SHIRRING TAPE

Shirring tape contains string or cording rows that are pulled to evenly gather fabric. Use shirring tape to create non-stretchy decorative shirring for home-dec projects, such as curtains.

Cut the shirring tape to the needed length for the desired shirred area. Position the shirring tape along the designated area; pin. (If shirring a curtain upper edge, stitch the rod pocket before shirring the fabric.) If the shirring

Shirring Supplies

Use these tools to shirr with ease.

Shirring Tape (A): Shirring tape is available in several widths to easily create various shirring effects on curtains and drapes.

Elastic Thread (B): Use narrow elastic thread suitable for machine sewing. Elastic thread is available in white, black and a few colors, so select the thread color that matches most closely with the chosen fabric.

Shirring feet (C): Machine manufacturers carry a variety of specialty machine and serger feet that automatically gather and shirr the fabric as you stitch. Consult your machine dealer to find shirring feet available for your machine.

Removable Fabric Marker (D): Use a removable fabric marker or tailor's chalk to evenly mark shirring lines.

tape is fusible, adhere according to the manufacturer's instructions. Stitch along the shirring-tape long edges, and then stitch between each cording row (9).

Pull the cording at each shirring-tape raw short end, evenly distributing the fabric (10). Be careful not to pull the cording out of the shirring tape casing. Pull the cording to create the desired fabric fullness, and then knot and trim the cords on the fabric wrong side (11).

SOURCES

Baby Lock provided the gathering foot: babylock.com.

Gütermann carries black and white elastic thread: guetermann.com.

Husqvarna Viking provided the gathering foot: (800) 446-2333, husqvarnaviking.com.

Prym Consumer USA, Inc. provided the tailor's marking tool: dritz.com.

Singer provided the serger shirring foot: (800) 474-6437, singerco.com.

Wrights provided the Magic Curtain Tape: (877) 588-2700, wrights.com.

7 PLACES TO PUCKER UP

Shirring adds a cute and feminine touch to projects. Check out these ideas for shirring placement:

1. Shirr the bodice of a casual sundress or beach cover-up. Elastic shirring snugly hugs the body, so the dress can be strapless or have narrow spaghetti straps.

2. Add a few rows of elastic shirring to a sleeve lower edge to create a puffed effect.

3. Shirr a curtain-panel upper edge, or stitch rows of vertical shirring down a window shade panel for a decorative effect.

4. Add shaping to a tunic or loose dress by shirring a small fabric section at the center front and center back below the bust.

5. To create an eye-catching throw pillow, stitch rows of non-stretchy shirring on a fabric panel. Evenly trim the shirred panel edges to the desired pillow size, and then use it as the throw-pillow cover front panel. For full instructions to stitch a shirred pillow, purchase the digital edition of *Sew Simple,* Volume 4 at quiltand-sewshop.com

6. Stitch a comfy, pull-on A-line skirt for a woman or little girl by stitching several shirring rows along the waistline edge.

7. Quickly create a trendy scarf by stitching shirring rows along a long fabric rectangle. Turn to "Pucker Up" on page 4 for instructions.

A SHORE THING

by Carol Zentgraf

Make a pull-over poncho for a seaside vacation using sheer silk or other lightweight fabric. Adjust the neckline and body for a custom fit.

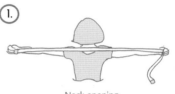

1.

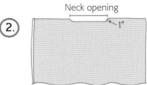

2. Neck opening
1"

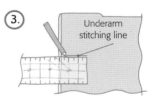

3. Underarm stitching line

SUPPLIES

1 yard of 58"-wide silk or other lightweight fabric

Thread: coordinating all-purpose & serger (See "Source.")

Tape

Fabric pencil

Clear ruler

Rotary cutting system

Serger (optional)

CUT IT

Along one selvage edge, tape the fabric to the gridded cutting mat aligned with one horizontal line. Fold the fabric in half, aligning the remaining selvage with the taped edge. Ensure the crosswise grain is perpendicular to the selvages and tape the remaining edge to the cutting mat.

Using a clear ruler, cut one fabric short edge along a vertical gridline to create 90° corners at the upper and lower edge. Measure across your back and shoulders from wrist to wrist, record (1). Cut the remaining poncho short edge according to the recorded measurement.

Determine the desired neck-opening width. The featured project has a total neck-opening width of 16¼". Using a rotary cutter and centering the opening along the fold, cut the neck opening 1" from the fold, tapering up at each end (2).

SEW IT

Thread the serger with coordinating thread and set it for a rolled edge.

Serge the poncho perimeter and neckline edges, or double-fold the edges ¼" toward the wrong side, and then stitch close to the first fold.

Place the poncho over your head and center it on your shoulders. Determine where you want the underarm sleeve stitching to end, pin mark. The featured project has underarm sleeve stitching ending 11" from the outer edges. Remove the poncho and fold it in half, aligning the edges. Using a chalk pencil, mark the underarm stitching line, pin (3). Repeat to mark the opposite side.

Beginning at the side, stitch each underarm following the marked line. ✪

SOURCE

Coats & Clark provided the Dual Duty sewing and serger thread: coatsandclark.com.

FULL CIRCLE FASHION

by Beth Bradley

A circle skirt is a fun and flirty summer staple that you'll want to make again and again. Draft your own pattern using your waist measurement and a little bit of simple geometry.

SUPPLIES

2½ yards of 60"-wide lightweight print fabric (See "Sources.")

2½ yards of lightweight lining fabric

One 9"-long invisible zipper

1 package of 1"- to 2½"-wide twill tape

All-purpose thread

Butcher paper or pattern tracing cloth

(at least 30" square; see "Sources.")

Hook and eye

Calculator

Clear ruler and French curve

Note: Use ½" seam allowances. The finished skirt is 21" long; add or subtract length as desired.

MEASURE IT

Take your waist measurement; record. To find the waist circumference, add 2" to the measurement to account for seam allowances, and then subtract 1" to account for the fabric stretching at the waistline. For example, if the measurement is 27", the resulting circumference is 28".

Divide the circumference by 3.14 (pi) to find the diameter. Round the number to the nearest tenth. For a 28" circumference, the diameter is rounded to 8.9".

Divide the diameter by two to find the radius, and then round to the nearest tenth. For an 8.9" diameter, the radius is 4.5", or 4½". Record the radius.

DRAFT IT

Place a large piece of paper or pattern tracing cloth on a flat work surface. Square two edges to create an exact 90° at one upper corner.

Measure and mark the radius length from the corner along one edge. Repeat to mark the radius measurement along the adjacent edge.

Make several marks denoting the radius length from the corner to create a quarter-circle. Connect the marks using a French curve. This is the waistline.

To draw the skirt hem, measure and mark a second curve 22" from the first curve. Label the pattern "Front" and draw an arrow along the center-front line to indicate that the pattern will be cut on the fold (1).

Trace the front pattern onto a second sheet of paper. Label the traced pattern "Back" and draw an arrow along the center-back line to indicate that the pattern will be cut on the fold.

(TiP)

Much of the circle skirt fabric will be on the bias, which tends to grow and stretch. Allow the skirt to hang overnight before hemming to allow for any distortion to occur.

(TiP)

To automatically convert the radius to inches without doing any calculations, go to sewitallmag.com to find a link to a converter

Math Class

Brush up on a few simple math principles to draft the pattern (A):

Circumference: Circle perimeter measurement.

Diameter: Measurement across the circle center.

Radius: 1/2 the diameter. For the circle skirt, the radius measurement is used to draft the waistline.

Pi: The ratio of any circle's circumference (C) to its diameter (d), written as Pi = C/d. For any circle, pi = 3.14. Use this formula to find any circle's radius.

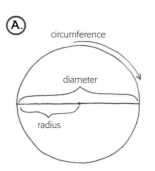

To allow the skirt front to lay flat over the midsection, mark 3/8" below the center-front upper corner. Use the French curve to connect the mark to the original waistline curve. To allow extra length in the skirt back (for the derriere), mark 3/8" above the center-front upper corner. Use the French curve to connect the mark to the original waistline curve (2).

CUT IT

Cut out the patterns.

Cut one skirt front and back each from the fabric and lining.

Cut a length of twill tape equal to the waist circumference, plus 1".

SEW IT

Use 1/2" seam allowances unless otherwise noted.

Independently staystitch the skirt and lining pieces 3/8" from the upper edge. Stitch each piece from one side edge to the center, and then repeat to stitch from the opposite side edge to the center.

With right sides together, stitch the skirt and lining right side seams; press open.

Mark the lining left skirt edges 8" below the upper edge to indicate the zipper opening. Stitch the lining left side seam from the lower edge to the mark (3).

Install the zipper in the skirt left side, following the manufacturer's instructions; stitch the side seam.

Serge- or zigzag-finish the seams, and then hang the skirt and lining overnight.

Try on the skirt to check for distortion at the hem. Measure from the floor to the skirt hem using a yardstick. If the skirt isn't the same length all around, trim away fabric as necessary.

Trim 1/4" from the skirt and lining upper edges.

Align the skirt and lining with wrong sides together, matching the waistline edges; baste or pin the layers.

Fold the twill tape ends 1/2" toward the wrong side; press. Fold the twill tape in half lengthwise with wrong sides together; press.

Beginning at the front-left upper edge, position the twill tape along the waistline, enclosing the skirt and lining raw edges in the twill tape fold; pin generously (4).

With the skirt right side up, stitch close to the twill tape lower edge, catching all layers in the stitching.

To hem the skirt, staystitch 1/4" from the lower edge. Fold the lower edge toward the wrong side along the stitching line, and then fold 1/4" again to enclose the raw edge; pin. Stitch close to the first fold. Repeat to hem the lining.

FINISH

Slipstitch the lining side opening to the zipper tape, and then hand stitch the hook and eye at the zipper upper edge. ✪

SOURCE

Fabric.com carries Pattern Ease tracing material: (888) 455-2940, fabric.com.

Westminster Fibers provided the Anna Maria Horner Little Folks voile fabric: (866) 907-3305, freespiritfabric.com.

1.
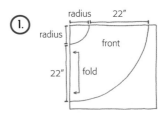

2.
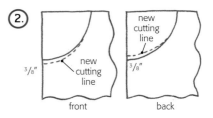

3.
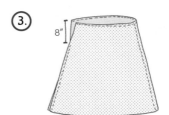

4.

BUBBLE SKIRT

by Joi Mahon

Make a fashionable and flirty bubble skirt using your favorite fabrics.

CHOOSE IT

For best results, use print cotton fabric, denim, taffeta or any fabric with body. Launder taffeta after construction to soften the appearance. Bubble skirts are especially striking when made using print cotton fabric, such as dots or plaid.

MEASURE IT

Using a soft tape measure, measure around your natural waist. Add 1" to the measurement; record. Cut one elastic length according to the recorded measurement.

Measure just above the fullest part of your hips. Add 1" to the measurement; record. Cut one elastic length according to the recorded measurement.

CUT IT

Refer to the following measurements, which include excess fabric to produce the bubble effect. From the fabric, cut the skirt according to the required length x the fabric width.

(TiP)

Add a fashion label to the waistband wrong side to help you remember which end is the waistband and which is the hip band. See "Source" for free fashion labels.

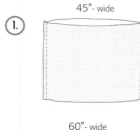

45"- wide

1.

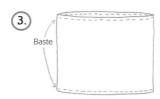

3.

Baste

60"- wide

2.

4.

Skirt Size	Desired Length	Cut
Child	Mid-thigh	21" long
Child	Knee	24" long
Adult	Mid-thigh	29" long
Adult	Knee	36" long

If using 45"-wide fabric, cut the fabric in half lengthwise to create two 1-yard rectangles. If using 60"-wide fabric, don't cut the fabric. Note: The 45"-wide fabric creates a fuller skirt around the body. For less fullness, trim excess fabric later in the construction process, if desired.

SEW IT

Use ½" seam allowances unless otherwise noted.

If using 45"-wide fabric, align the fabric rectangles with right sides together; pin, and then stitch the short edges to create two side seams (1). Serge- or zigzag-finish the seams. (The fabric short ends are the fabric selvages.)

If using 60"-wide fabric, fold the fabric widthwise with right sides together; pin, and then stitch the open short end, creating one center-back seam (2). Serge- or zigzag-finish the seams. (The fabric short ends are the fabric selvages.)

Select a long basting stitch on the machine. Stitch the skirt long edges, making sure not to stitch the fabric layers together (3).

Align the waist-elastic short ends with right sides together; pin, and then stitch. Serge- or zigzag-finish the ends. Repeat to stitch the hip elastic.

Fold the waist elastic in half widthwise; mark the center. Fold the short ends toward the center mark; mark to indicate four equal parts. Repeat to mark the hip elastic.

Quarter-mark each skirt short end in the same manner as for the elastic (4). Note: If using directional fabric, note the waist end and hip end.

With right sides together, align the waist elastic with the skirt waistline, matching the marks; pin. With right sides together, align the hip elastic with the opposite skirt edge, matching the marks; pin.

Install a size 80/14 needle into the machine. Select a 3.5mm-wide zigzag or overlock stitch. Stitch the waistline, gathering the fabric to match the elastic by gently pulling the basting thread. There's no need to stretch the elastic while stitching. Pull the basting thread in small increments to ensure even gathers. Repeat to stitch the opposite skirt end. Serge- or zigzag-finish the seams.

WEAR IT

Step into the skirt. Pull the waistband toward your waist.

Pull the lower elastic above the fullest part of the hips, tucking the elastic underneath the fabric. The hip elastic is slightly larger than the waist elastic, so it won't slip while wearing. ✪

SOURCE

Dress Forms Design Studio, LLC provided the wide elastic and free fashion label: (712) 239-9921, dressformsdesign.com.

Your Style

Use these styling tips to customize the look of your bubble skirt:

- To shorten the skirt, roll the hip elastic toward the right side to take up length.

- To lengthen the skirt, slide the hip elastic toward your hips. Tack the elastic along the side seams so it won't slide, if necessary. Or use decorative safety pins to secure the longer length on the skirt right side.

- Allow the hip elastic to hang around the calves or ankles for a long skirt.

- Pull the waist elastic above the bust underneath the arms for a strapless dress. Add ribbon straps if desired.

- Create a smaller version for an infant by adjusting the length and fullness measurements. Measure the child's waist circumference and adjust the measurements accordingly.

- Embellish the waistband with fabric flowers, screen printed shapes, hot-fix crystals or other embellishments for added flair.

PETAL
TO THE METAL

by Cathie Filian

Deconstruct zippers and
then reconstruct them
into a beautiful brooch.

Check out *Sew It All* episode 205, "Hipper Zippers" and watch Cathie Filian construct the featured brooch. Visit sewitalltv.com and sew.tv for more information.

SUPPLIES

Two 24"-long all-purpose zippers

One 24"-long contrasting all-purpose zipper

Two 1³/₄"-diameter felt circles

All-purpose thread

Hand sewing needle

1¹/₂"-long pin back

Fabric glue (optional)

CUT IT

Cut off each zipper stop. Separate each zipper, and then remove the pulls.

Cut the two matching zippers into eight 4"-long pieces, one 5"-long piece and one 7"-long piece. Cut the contrasting zipper into eight 3"-long pieces.

Thread a hand sewing needle with a strand of all-purpose thread; double-knot the thread end. Form a loop with one 4"-long zipper piece, overlapping the ends. Whipstitch the zipper ends to secure (1). Repeat to stitch the remaining 4"- and 3"-long zipper pieces, forming petals.

Position the large petals along one felt-circle right side, orienting the petal lower edges toward the circle center and evenly spacing the petals. Overlap the petals, if necessary.

Whipstitch the petal lower edges to secure (2). Repeat to stitch the small petals over the large petals.

Hand stitch a long running stitch along the tape straight edge of the 5"-long zipper piece, leaving a long thread tail. Pull the thread end to form the tape into a flat coil (3). Align the zipper tape short ends with right sides together; hand stitch to secure. Position the coil over the flower center; hand stitch or glue to secure.

Roll up the 7"-long zipper piece into a tight rosette; hand stitch the lower-tape edge through all layers to secure (4). Position the rosette over the coil center with the zipper teeth right side up; hand stitch or glue to the felt to secure.

Center the pin back on the remaining felt-circle right side; hand stitch the pin to secure. Align the felt circles with wrong sides together; whipstitch the perimeter or glue the layers together. ❂

SOURCES

Beacon Fabric & Notions carries zippers: (800) 713-8157, beaconfabric.com.

Coats & Clark provided Dual Duty all-purpose thread, Dual Duty XP heavyweight thread and the zippers: (800) 648-1479, coatsandclark.com.

ZipperStop carries zippers: (888) 947-7872, zipperstop.com.

(TiP)

Adjust the petal lengths and experiment by creating different zipper shapes for the flower center, if desired.

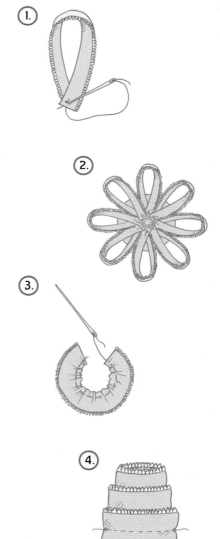

1.

2.

3.

4.

GATHER ROUND

by Ellen March

Ever wonder what to do with a fun fabric that you don't necessarily want to use for an entire garment? Make fabric jewelry! The featured necklace only takes about 20 minutes to construct.

SUPPLIES

1½"x44" strip of print fabric cut on the bias

22"-long piece of ⁶/₃₂" cording

All-purpose thread

Hand sewing needle

Safety pin

Tube turner, chopstick or knitting needle

Wear the necklace as a headband for an entirely new look!

SEW IT

Fold one bias strip end ½" toward the wrong side; press. Fold the strip in half lengthwise with right sides together; press. Stitch the long edge.

Turn the tube right side out using a tube turner, chopstick or knitting needle.

Stitch back and forth along each cording end several times to flatten. Pin a safety pin through one cording end, anchoring the pin through the stitching lines.

Insert the safety pin through the tube folded end (1). Use the pin to guide the cording through the tube,

gathering the fabric slightly to expose both cording ends.

Remove the safety pin. Overlap the cording ends and stitch back and forth across the ends to secure (2).

Insert the tube raw end ¼" to ½" into the tube folded end, aligning the seams.

Slipstitch the tube ends along the fold, concealing the raw end.

Distribute the gathers along the cording, as desired. ✪

1.

2.

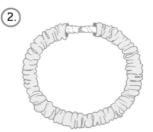

TOTALLY TUBULAR

Learn stress-free tube-turning techniques to create fabric tubes for garment or purse straps, jewelry, waistbands and more.

IN THE TUBE

Create a tube from a fabric strip that's twice the desired finished tube width plus the seam allowance. The wider the tube, the easier it is to turn right side out.

Create open or closed tubes based on the chosen project. Fold a fabric strip in half lengthwise with right sides together. To create an open tube, stitch the long edge. To create a closed tube, stitch the long edge and one short end.

Cut fabric strips on the lengthwise, crosswise or bias grain to accommodate different tube widths. Create tubes from woven or knit fabric.

- Lengthwise grain fabric strips are stable, have the least amount of stretch and are best for straight tubes. Don't cut narrow tubes on the lengthwise grain because there's not enough stretch to facilitate turning.

- Crosswise grain fabric strips have slightly more stretch and are best for straight tubes and gentle curves.

- Bias fabric strips have the most stretch and are best for curved and narrow tubes because the stretch makes turning and shaping the tube easier.

- Knit fabric strips have the most stretch, depending on the knit and type, and are best for making waistline drawstrings.

Use a pencil or chopstick for turning closed tubes.

Place the pencil eraser or chopstick blunt end into the closed-tube short end, and then pull ½" of the fabric over the pencil or chopstick end.

Push the pencil or chopstick through the tube toward the open short end, while pulling the fabric back over the tool in the opposite direction (2). Remove the pencil or chopstick. ✪

Tube Tips

Follow these tips for terrific tubes every time.

- Cut corduroy tubes lengthwise along the wales for easier turning.

- Cut a tube 2" to 3" longer than needed and decrease the seam allowance 2" to 3" from the end, creating a wider opening so a tube turner tool easily fits into the tube.

- Insert cording into a tube for definition and stability. Or increase the fabric-strip seam allowance to match the tube width. The seam allowance acts as a light filler for added stability when the tube is turned right side out.

- Cut a cardboard piece slightly narrower than the tube. Insert the cardboard into the tube to aid in pressing the tube flat without twisting.

IN THE LOOP

by Beth Bradley

Stitch a super simple infinity scarf to add color to a dull winter day. The scarf takes only minutes to construct and you can wear it in a variety of creative ways.

5 Ways to Wear

1. **Basic Cowl:** Wrap the scarf twice around your neck; evenly adjust the loops.

2. **Double Cowl**: Wrap the scarf twice around your neck, and then pull one loop to drape longer than the other.

3. **Shawl**: Place the scarf around your shoulders, and then adjust the fabric to drape over your upper arms.

4. **Hood**: Wrap the scarf twice around your neck, and then pull one loop over the back of your head.

5. **Bolero:** Pull your arms through the loop from behind and drape the fabric over your shoulders.

SUPPLIES

14"x60" strip each of 2 coordinating knit fabrics

All-purpose thread

Hand sewing needle

Serger (optional)

SEW IT

Align the strips with right sides together; pin.

Set the serger to a 3-thread overlock stitch. If using a conventional sewing machine, select a narrow zigzag stitch. Stitch the strip long edges, leaving a 4" opening along one edge for turning. Turn the strip right side out.

Turn the strip inside itself toward the wrong side, pulling the fabric through the tube until the short ends are aligned with right sides together. Align the long seams; pin, and then stitch the short ends (1).

Turn the scarf right side out through the opening. Slipstitch the opening closed. ✣

(TiP)
To identify a knit fabric's right and wrong sides, stretch a small section; the raw edge will roll toward the wrong side.

Style Options

Follow these tips to change the look of your scarf:

• To create a longer scarf with even more style options, piece fabric strips along the short ends to achieve the desired length.

• For a glamorous touch, stitch a length of sequined or beaded trim along one strip lengthwise center before constructing the scarf.

• Add interest by using a drapey sweater-knit fabric or a textured knit.

• For a breezy summer scarf, select a lightweight woven fabric, such as gauze or voile.

• Make a monochromatic scarf by using the same fabric for both layers. Or add pop by combining two coordinating prints, such as a stripe and a floral print.

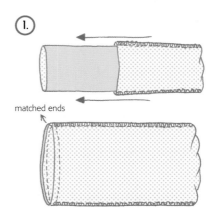

matched ends

HAIR FLAIR
by Andrea DeHart

Use fabric from your stash to create cute headbands. Vary the fabric colors to coordinate with different outfits or to match your personal style.

HANKIE HEADBAND
SUPPLIES

2 fat quarters of cotton fabric

Headband insert

All-purpose thread

Hand sewing needle

Pattern paper or newspaper

MEASURE IT

Measure the headband insert length and width; record. Draw a rectangle on a piece of pattern paper according to the recorded dimensions.

Measure 10" below the rectangle center for an adult headband or 8" below the rectangle center for a child headband; mark. Draw lines to connect each rectangle lower edge corner with

the mark (1). Add ½" seam allowances to all sides, and then cut out the pattern.

SEW IT

Use ½" seam allowances.

Cut one hankie from each fat quarter. Stitch the hankies with right sides together, leaving one short end open for turning.

Turn the hankie right side out; press. Fold the raw edges ½" toward the wrong side; press, and then pin. Edgestitch the hankie perimeter, leaving the opening free.

Add ½" to the headband width measurement to account for ease; record. Stitch a line parallel to the hankie upper edge, according to the recorded measurement. For example, the featured headband is ³⁄₈" wide, so the stitching is ⁵⁄₈" from the hankie upper edge (2).

FINISH IT

Thread the headband insert through the hankie opening, and then whipstitch the opening closed.

FLOWER HEADBAND
SUPPLIES

Felt scraps

Headband insert

³⁄₈"-diameter button

Embroidery floss

Hand embroidery needle

Removable fabric marker

Craft glue or double-sided tape

CUT IT

Trace the "Hair Flair" templates from page 64 onto paper or card stock,

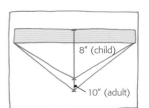

8" (child)

10" (adult)

⁵/₈" ⊢   open

(TiP)

If you can't find headband inserts, purchase inexpensive plastic headbands at a drugstore or thrift store.

cut out and label. Measure the headband insert length and width, and then add ¼" to the measurements; record.

From the felt, cut two rectangles according to the recorded measurements, one small flower, one base flower and one center. Transfer the pattern marks.

SEW IT

Using craft glue or double-sided tape, adhere one felt strip to the headband right side. Repeat to adhere the remaining felt strip to the headband wrong side. Let the glue dry, if using.

Thread a hand embroidery needle with three strands of floss. Beginning at one headband short edge, blanket stitch or whipstitch the perimeter.

Thread a hand embroidery needle with one strand of floss; knot the end. Baste the small flower along the dotted line. Gently pull the thread to gather the flower; knot the end. Repeat to gather the large flower (3).

FINISH IT

Position the flower base on a flat work surface. Layer the large flower, then the small flower, then the flower center over the base. Center the button over the flower center. Hand stitch the button through all layers; knot the thread end.

Stitch the button to the flower center through all the layers; tie the end.

Hand stitch the flower backside to the headband, where desired.

BUTTON BAUBLE HEADBAND
SUPPLIES

Headband insert

Ribbon (¼" wider than headband insert)

Coordinating buttons

Hand sewing needle

All-purpose thread

CUT IT

Measure the headband length, and then add ¼" to the measurement. Double the measurement; record. Cut one ribbon strip according to the recorded measurement.

SEW IT

Fold the ribbon in half widthwise with right sides together; pin. Fold the short edges ¼" toward the wrong side; press, and then pin.

Edgestitch the ribbon long edges, leaving the ends free.

Thread the headband insert through one ribbon end, and then whipstitch the ends closed.

FINISH IT

Cluster several buttons along the headband upper edge, as desired. Hand stitch each button to the headband. ✪

ALL IN THE WRIST

by Nicki LaFoille

Stay cozy and fashionable in cold weather with custom-designed wrist warmers.

SUPPLIES

¼ yard of fleece fabric (See "Sources.")

Coordinating all-purpose thread

Hand sewing needle

Removable fabric marker or chalk

12" length of ¼"-wide decorative trim (optional)

SEW IT

Place your palm on a flat surface in a relaxed position. Measure the circumference of the heel of your hand at the widest point; add 1", and then record. Measure from your knuckles to the desired wrist-warmer lower edge; add 3", and then record.

Cut two fleece rectangles according to the recorded dimensions. To create the featured project, cut two 9"x10" rectangles. Designate one short edge as the upper edge and the remaining short edge as the lower edge.

Fold each short edge ¼" toward the wrong side; pin, and then stitch close to the fold. Fold the wrist warmer in half lengthwise with right sides together, aligning the long edges. Using a removable fabric marker or chalk, mark the raw edge ¾" and 2½" below the upper edge (1).

Unfold the wrist warmer. Mark the lengthwise center. Baste the centerline, leaving long thread tails at the stitching beginning and end. Carefully pull the bobbin thread tails to evenly gather the

(TiP)

For less bulk at the wrist, only baste and gather 2″ to 3″ from the lower edge. Or, taper the fleece below the second mark. Pin the seam allowance and make sure your hand will still fit through before stitching.

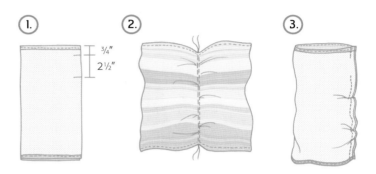

wrist warmer to the desired length. Knot the needle and bobbin thread tails at the stitching beginning and end to secure the gathers.

Set the machine to a medium stitch length. Stitch over the basting, backstitching at the beginning and end (2). Remove the basting if desired.

With right sides together, fold the wrist warmer in half lengthwise, aligning the long raw edges. Baste the seam below the lower mark using a ¼″ seam allowance. Baste again using a ½″ seam allowance to avoid breaking the basting thread when gathering.

Pull the bobbin thread tails to evenly gather the fleece to the desired length. Note: The featured wrist warmers are 7¾″ long. Knot the thread ends at the stitching beginning and end to secure the gathers. Set the machine to a medium stitch length. Stitch the seam using a ½″ seam allowance, backstitching at the beginning and end. Remove the basting.

Using a ⅝″ seam allowance, stitch from the upper mark to the upper edge; press open the seam (3).

Hand stitch the thumb-opening seam allowances to the wrist warmer.

If desired, hand stitch trim along the outer gathering line. ✪

SOURCES

Fabric.com provided the fleece: (888) 455-2940, fabric.com.

Janome provided the Jem Platinum 760 sewing machine used to construct the project: janome.com.

Change Up

Design your own wrist warmers using these tips for inspiration.

• **Stitch pretty wrist warmers** for any season by using different fabrics. Choose lace, silk or chiffon for a spring or summer accessory. If using fabric with less stretch, stitch an upper- and lower-edge casing and insert a thin elastic band.

• **Stitch a contrasting fabric** inset along the outer edge. Divide the wrist warmer circumference in half. Subtract the desired inset width evenly from each panel. Add seam allowances to each new edge. Stitch following the instructions at left (A). Gather the inset through the center, or at each seamline, if desired.

• **Attach ribbon** or other trim to the upper and/or lower edges (B).

• **Use a worn sweatshirt** to stitch a pair of cozy wrist warmers. Simply cut the required dimensions from the sweatshirt body. If using an open knit sweatshirt, serge- or zigzag-finish the fabric raw edges to prevent raveling before constructing.

Rainy Day TOTE

by Carol Zentgraf

Make a designer-inspired laminated tote that keeps your items dry and is easily wiped clean.

SUPPLIES

⅔ yard of laminated cotton fabric

⅝ yard of coordinating cotton fabric

1 yard of 20"-wide fusible woven interfacing

2½ yards of ½"-wide fusible web tape

Removable fabric marker

Press cloth

CUT IT

From the laminated cotton, cut two 18"x19" rectangles for the tote and two 2½"x22" strips for the straps.

From the cotton, cut two 18"x19" rectangles for the lining.

From the interfacing, cut two 18"x19" rectangles.

SEW IT

Use ½" seam allowances. The finished tote measurements are 5"x13"x17".

With right sides together, stitch the tote rectangles along one short edge and both long edges. Press open the seams using a press cloth.

To box the corners, align one side seam with the lower-edge seam. Measure 5" below the corner; mark a horizontal line using a removable fabric marker. Stitch along the line. Trim off the corner (1). Repeat to box the remaining corner. Turn the bag right side out.

Fuse the interfacing rectangles to the lining rectangle wrong sides, following the manufacturer's instructions.

With right sides together, stitch the lining rectangles along one short edge and both long edges, leaving a 6" opening along the short edge for turning. Press open the seams. Don't turn the lining right side out. Box the lining corners, following the tote instructions.

Position one strap right side down on a flat work surface. Position one 22"-long fusible web tape piece along one strip long edge on the wrong side; press using a press cloth. Repeat to adhere a second fusible web tape piece to the opposite long edge. Remove the paper backing, and then fold the strip long edges toward the center; press using a press cloth to adhere (2). Fold the strip in half lengthwise; topstitch the long edges. Repeat to stitch the remaining strap.

With raw edges aligned and right sides together, position each strap end 5" from each side seam along one tote side; baste. Repeat to baste the remaining strap to the opposite tote side.

FINISH IT

Place the tote inside the lining with right sides together, matching the side seams and upper edges. Pin, and then stitch the upper edge.

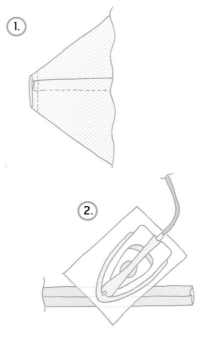

Turn the tote right side out through the lining opening. Slipstitch the lining opening closed. Push the lining into the tote. Finger-press the upper edge, and then topstitch ½" from the upper edge. ✪

SOURCES

Pellon provided Shape-Flex interfacing: (800) 233-5275, pellonideas.com.

The Warm Company provided Steam-A-Seam 2 paper-backed fusible web: (425) 248-2424, warmcompany.com.

Westminster Fibers provided the Ty Pennington Moorish Chartreuse laminated cotton and Water Flower Gray cotton fabrics: (866) 907-3305, westminsterfibers.com.

MUSIC MATES

by Beth Bradley

Protect your mp3 player in a
quick-to-make laminated cotton
case with a handy key ring.

Supplies listed are enough to make one 2½" square case.

6" square of laminated cotton (See "Sources.")

3"x6" rectangle of flannel or fleece

All-purpose thread (See "Sources.")

5" length of ½"-wide elastic

Key ring

Paper clips

SEW IT

Use ¼" seam allowances.

From the laminated cotton, cut one 3"x6" rectangle for the case and one 1"x3" strip for the key-ring tab.

Fold the strip long edges to abut along the center, and then fold it in half lengthwise. Edgestitch the long open edge.

With right sides together, align the laminated cotton and flannel rectangles; pin within the seam allowance.

Fold the elastic in half widthwise, and then place the elastic between the rectangles centered along one short edge. Allow the elastic ends to extend ½" beyond the short edge; pin.

Stitch the rectangle perimeter, leaving a 1" opening along one long edge for turning. Clip the corners, and then turn the rectangle right side out. Fold the opening edges toward the wrong side. Press from the flannel side using a cool iron.

Fold the rectangle in half widthwise with the laminated cotton facing out Fold the strip in half widthwise. To create the key-ring tab, position the folded strip between the case layers along one side, ½" below the upper edge, allowing about ⅜" of the strip to extend beyond the case for the key ring. Paper clip the case edges together.

Stitch the case sides, backstitching at the beginning and end and catching the tab in the stitching.

FINISH IT

Slide the key ring onto the tab. To use the case, wind the earbud cord around the case and secure it with the elastic loop. ❂

SOURCES

Coats & Clark provided the Double Duty XP all-purpose thread: (800) 648-1479, coatsandclark.com.

Connecting Threads provided the laminated cotton fabric: (800) 574-6454, connectingthreads.com.

Case by Case

Make a larger laminated cotton case to fit a cell phone or full-size mp3 player.

• **Measure the device length and width,** and then add ½" to each measurement; record. Cut two rectangles each from laminated cotton and flannel according to the recorded measurement.

• **To determine the elastic measurement,** double the device length, and then subtract 1".

• **Align the laminated cotton rectangles,** and then stitch the sides and lower edges using ¼" seam allowances. Repeat to stitch the flannel rectangles, but leave a 1½" opening along the lower edge for turning. Clip the laminated cotton case corners and then turn it right side out; don't turn the flannel case right side out.

• **Place the laminated cotton case** in the flannel case with right sides together, aligning the seams and upper edges. Fold the elastic in half widthwise, and then place it between the case layers, centering the ends along one side; pin.

• **Stitch the case upper edge.** Turn the case right side out through the flannel opening, and then push the flannel into the laminated cotton case. Slipstitch the opening closed.

CRAFT CADDY

Carry craft supplies and sewing notions in a sturdy yet lightweight caddy equipped with plenty of pockets.

by Beth Bradley

Purchase the "Craft Caddy" fabric kit at shopsewitall.com to create your own handy tote!

SUPPLIES

½ yard each of three coordinating laminated cotton fabrics (A, B & C; see "Sources")

Paper clips or masking tape

Chalk marker

Size 80/12 sharp or microfiber needle (optional)

Press cloth (optional)

CUT IT

Lay out the fabrics on a large flat surface a few hours before cutting to allow creases to relax. Never press directly on the laminated fabric surface, as the iron's heat melts the vinyl coating. If pressing is necessary, use a press cloth and a low heat setting.

From fabric A, cut two 11"x17" rectangles for the caddy exterior and two 10"x17" rectangles for the inner pockets.

From fabric B, cut two 11"x17" rectangles for the caddy interior and two 10"x17" rectangles for the large outer pockets.

From fabric C, cut two 7"x17" rectangles for the small outer pockets and two 4½"x14" rectangles for the handles.

SEW IT

Use a 3mm-long straight stitch and ½" seam allowances unless otherwise noted.

With wrong sides together, fold one fabric-B pocket in half lengthwise. Stitch the long open edge. Turn the pocket right side out, and then finger-press flat or use an iron and press cloth. Topstitch the pocket folded edge using an ⅛" seam allowance (1). Repeat to construct and topstitch the remaining fabric-A, -B and -C pockets.

Position one fabric-A exterior rectangle right side up on flat work surface, designating one long edge as the upper edge. Using a chalk marker, draw a line 3" above and parallel to the rectangle lower edge.

Position one fabric-B pocket over the fabric-A rectangle, aligning the pocket lower (not topstitched) edge with the marked line; tape or paper clip in place. Position one fabric-C pocket over the fabric-B pocket, aligning the fabric-C pocket lower edge with the marked line; tape or paper clip in place. Topstitch the pocket lower edge through all layers using an ⅛" seam allowance (2). Repeat to construct the remaining caddy exterior.

To indicate the outer-pocket divider stitching, draw a vertical line on the pockets 5½" from each side. Stitch along each line through all layers (3).

Align the exterior rectangles with right sides together; paper clip or tape in place. Stitch the sides and lower edge.

To box the exterior lower corners, pinch one lower corner with right sides together, aligning the side and lower seams. Stitch through all layers 3" from the corner, and then trim the corner ½" from the stitching (4). Repeat to box and trim the remaining lower corner.

(TiP)

If you're experiencing skipped stitches when sewing laminated cotton, switch to a narrow sharp or microfiber needle. These needles have sharper points that easily penetrate the laminated surface.

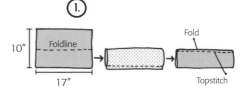

① 10" Foldline 17" Fold Topstitch

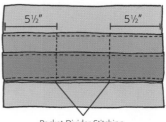

② Topstitch 3"

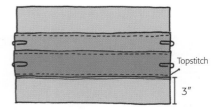

③ 5½" 5½" Pocket Divider Stitching

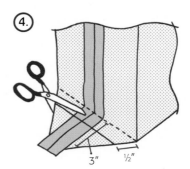

④ 3" ½"

Turn the caddy exterior right side out; finger-press or iron if necessary.

Position one fabric-B interior rectangle right side up on a flat work surface, designating one long edge as the upper edge. Using a chalk marker, draw a line 3" above and parallel to the rectangle lower edge.

Position one fabric-A pocket over the fabric-B rectangle, aligning the pocket lower edge with the marked line; tape or paper clip in place. Topstitch the pocket lower edge through all layers using an ⅛" seam allowance. Repeat to construct the remaining caddy interior.

To indicate the inner-pocket divider stitching, draw three evenly spaced vertical lines on the pockets. Stitch along each line through all layers.

Align the interior rectangles with right sides together; paper clip or tape in place. Stitch the sides and lower

edge, leaving a 4" opening along the lower edge for turning. Box and trim the interior lower corners in the same manner as the caddy exterior. Don't turn the caddy interior right side out.

To construct the handles, fold each handle rectangle in half lengthwise with right sides together. Stitch each handle long open edge, and then turn each handle right side out; finger-press or iron. Topstitch each handle long edge using an ⅛" seam allowance.

Mark each handle 4½" from each short edge. Fold each handle in half lengthwise, and then stitch between the marks using an ⅛" seam allowance (5).

Mark the caddy-exterior right-side upper edge 5" from each side seam to indicate the handle placements. With the handle wrong side facing up, center one handle end over each mark; paper clip in place (6).

With right sides together, place the caddy exterior inside the caddy interior, aligning the upper edges and side seams. Paper clip the upper edges, and then stitch.

Gently turn the caddy right side out through the interior lower-edge opening, and then push the interior caddy inside the exterior caddy. Finger-press or iron if needed. Align the interior-opening edges, and then edgestitch closed.

FINISH IT

Paper-clip the caddy upper edge to keep the layers neatly aligned, and then topstitch the upper edge using an ⅛" seam allowance. ✪

SOURCES

Coats & Clark provided the Double Duty XP all-purpose thread: (800) 648-1479, coatsandclark.com.

Westminster Fibers provided the Heather Bailey Freshcut Laminate fabrics: (866) 907-3305, www.westminsterfibers.com.

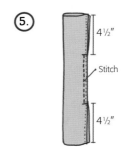

(5.)   4½"

Stitch

4½"

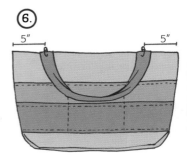

(6.)   5"   5"

(TiP)
Customize the caddy by adding or subtracting pockets or divider stitching lines according to your storage needs.

CUDDLE UP

by Sara Boughner

Make a cuddly baby blanket using super soft minkee fabric and a favorite print fabric. Double or triple the measurements to make a full-size blanket.

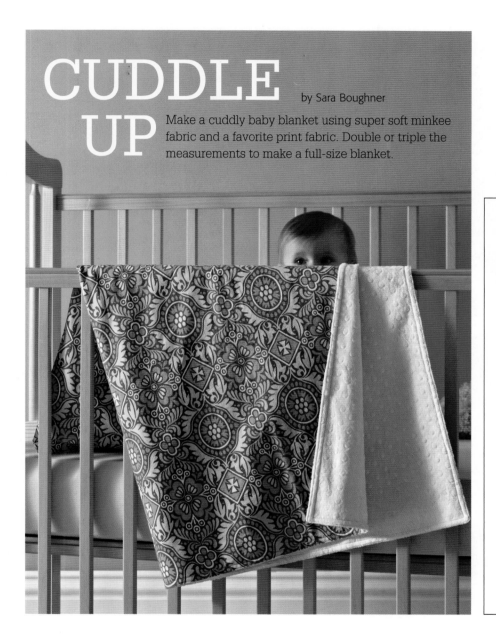

(TiP)

Cut both fabrics in the same direction to reduce unwanted stretching, as minkee fabric stretches against the grain, not selvage to selvage.

Minkee Minded

Minkee is a soft fabric that's easy to work with when you know the following tips:

• **Use a walking foot** when stitching minkee to prevent the fabric layers from shifting.

• **Don't iron minkee;** instead, finger-press open seams when necessary.

• **When cutting minkee,** have a lint roller handy, as minkee fibers shed when cut.

• **Minkee produces a lot of lint** in the throatplate, feed dogs and bobbin case, so clean them often.

• **Always test stitch on a fabric scrap** to ensure the stitch length is satisfactory. Minkee puckers when the stitch length is too short.

SUPPLIES

1 yard of print cotton fabric

1 yard of minkee fabric

Coordinating all-purpose thread

CUT IT

Prewash and dry the fabric. Cut one 34"x40" rectangle from each fabric.

SEW IT

Align the rectangles with right sides together; generously pin the perimeter.

Using a ½" seam allowance, stitch the perimeter, leaving a 4" opening along one edge for turning.

For added durability, serge- or zigzag-finish the seam allowances.

Reinforce the corners by backstitching at the beginning and end of the stitching lines.

Turn the blanket right side out through the opening; press from the cotton side.

Fold the opening edges ½" toward the wrong side; press, and then pin.

FINISH IT

Edgestitch the blanket perimeter. Topstitch approximately ¼" inside the edgestitching. ✪

Square ONE

by Beth Bradley

Welcome a new addition to the family by stitching a simple, modern patchwork quilt using a mix of cheerful print fabrics.

SUPPLIES

Supplies listed are enough to make a 45"x60" quilt.

15 coordinating print-cotton fat quarters (See "Sources.")

3 yards of solid or print cotton fabric (backing; see "Sources")

½ yard of print cotton fabric (binding; see "Sources")

Crib-size low-loft cotton batting (See "Sources.")

Cotton quilting thread (See "Sources.")

Quilt basting spray (See "Sources.")

Rotary cutting system (See "Sources.")

Large safety pins

Hand quilting needle

PREP IT

Prewash the fabric; press.

Using the rotary cutting system, cut one 10" square, one 5" square, two 3"x5" rectangles and two 3"x10" rectangles from each fat quarter (1). Refer to "Rotary Cutting" on page 35.

Cut enough 2½"-wide strips from the binding fabric to equal 216" including ¼" seam allowances.

Set aside the large squares. Designate one small square for each set of 3"x5" and 3"x10" rectangles, mixing the colors and prints as desired. Position the small squares right side up on flat work surface, and then position sets of rectangles along the square edges until satisfied with the print and color combinations.

SEW IT

Use ¼" seam allowances.

To construct each small-square block, align one small-rectangle long edge with one small-square edge with right sides together; stitch. Stitch the remaining small rectangle to the opposite square edge. Press the seam allowances toward the darker fabric.

With right sides together, align one large rectangle with one pieced-panel long edge; stitch. Stitch the remaining large rectangle to the opposite panel edge (2). Press the seam allowances toward the darker fabric. Repeat to construct a total of 15 pieced blocks.

On a large flat work surface, arrange the pieced blocks and 10" squares in a layout of six rows and five columns. Alternate the pieced blocks and 10" squares, distributing the prints and colors until pleased with the arrangement (3).

To construct the quilt top, stitch the blocks in each row with right sides together. Press the seam allowances toward the darker fabrics.

Align the first and second rows with right sides together, matching the seams; pin and then stitch. Repeat to stitch each remaining row. Press the seam allowances toward the darker fabrics.

To create the quilt back, cut and piece the backing fabric as needed to create a 45"x60" rectangle.

(TiP)

Snap a picture of the quilt layout on your phone or digital camera to use for reference as you piece the quilt top.

1.
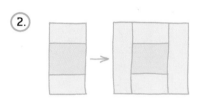

2.
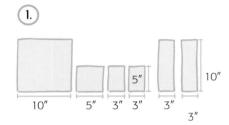

3.
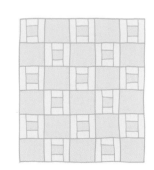

QUILT IT

Find a flat work surface large enough to accommodate the entire quilt. Spread out the batting, smoothing out any wrinkles or folds.

Apply basting spray to the batting surface, following the manufacturer's instructions. Layer the backing rectangle right side up over the batting, aligning the perimeter and smoothing out any wrinkles.

Turn the layers so the opposite batting side is facing up, and then apply basting spray to the batting surface. Layer the quilt top right side up over the batting, aligning the perimeters and smoothing out any wrinkles.

Beginning at the quilt center, pin a safety pin through all layers. Working from the center outward, continue pinning the layers, spacing the safety pins about a hand's width apart and smoothing all wrinkles.

Quilt the layers as desired. Refer to "Patchwork Primer" on page 36 for quilting options. The featured quilt is stitched in the ditch along each row and column seam and around each small square. The large squares are channel quilted using horizontal, vertical and diagonal lines spaced 1½" apart.

Evenly trim the fabric and batting layers along the quilt perimeter.

FINISH IT

With right sides together, piece the binding-strip short edges to create one continuous strip.

Fold one binding short end 1" toward the fabric wrong side. Fold the binding in half lengthwise with wrong sides together.

Position the binding short folded end along one quilt long edge with right sides together and raw edges aligned. Begin stitching through all layers 2" from the short folded end.

At each corner, raise the needle, rotate the quilt 90°, and fold the binding up and back down over itself, aligning the binding raw edge with the adjacent quilt edge to form a mitered corner. Lower the needle and continue stitching (4).

End the stitching 1" before the binding beginning. Trim the binding end to fit inside the beginning fold. Insert the raw end into the beginning fold (5). Continue stitching to finish attaching the binding.

Fold the binding toward the quilt back, enclosing the raw edges and covering the machine stitching. Slipstitch the binding fold to the quilt back, mitering each corner. ❂

SOURCES

Coats & Clark provided the quilting thread: (800) 648-1479, coatsandclark.com.

Connecting Threads provided the Hello Sunshine! fabric collection for the quilt top, backing and binding: (800) 574-6454, connectingthreads.com.

Fairfield provided the American Spirit Classic Cotton batting: (800) 980-8000, fairfieldworld.com.

Fiskars provided the Ergo Control Rotary Cutter: (866) 348- 5661, fiskars.com.

June Tailor carries Quilt Basting Spray: (262) 644-5288, junetailor.com.

(TiP)

To create a cozy throw or lap quilt rather than a baby quilt, use fabrics that match your living room or bedroom décor.

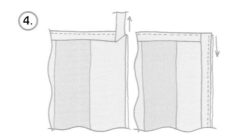

ROTARY CUTTING

by Beth Bradley

Rotary fabric cutters, mats and rulers help you cut fabric smoothly, straightly and evenly. You'll save time and energy using a rotary cutting system, especially when creating quilts and grading seams.

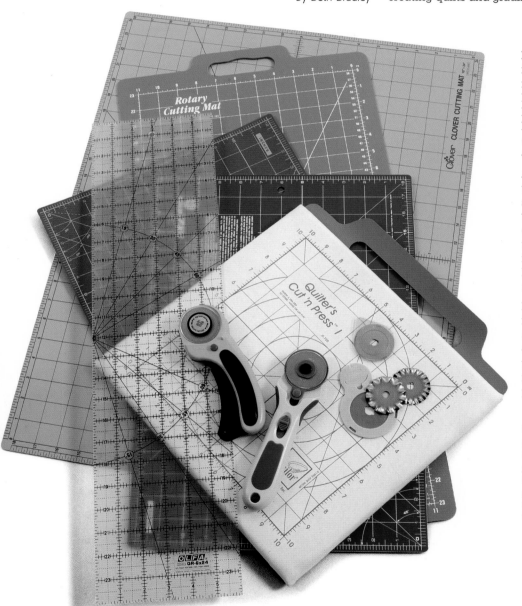

Rotary cutters are a definite must-have for cutting multiple fabric layers, precise measurements or decorative fabric edges. Don't fret if you're a lefty, as rotary cutters have different handle shapes designed for left- or right-handed use. Rotary cutters come in many sizes, but 18mm, 28mm, 45mm and 60mm are the most popular.

Always use a rotary cutting mat when using a rotary cutter. The mats are self-healing and blades won't damage them. Most mats have grids that provide a guide for fabric placement; however, don't use the grids as accurate measurements for cutting—that's what rulers are for. Don't leave your mat out in the heat, as it can warp the mat for good.

Rulers align the fabric and hold it firmly against the cutting mat for optimal accuracy. Most rotary rulers have 30°, 45° and 60° lines imprinted on them, so you can cut fabric at precise angles. Like rotary mats, keep your rulers in a safe place so they don't get scratched. ✲

SOURCES

Clover provided rotary cutters, rotary cutter blade refills and rotary cutting mats: (800) 233-1703, clover-usa.com.

June Tailor provided the Quilter's Cut 'n Press I and III and rotary cutting mats: (800) 844-5400, junetailor.com.

Olfa provided rotary cutters, scallop and pinking blades, square rulers and rotary cutting mats: (800) 962-6532, olfa.com.

(TiP)

Swap out your rotary blades to create unique edges.

PATCHWORK PRIMER

by Beth Bradley

Most people immediately think of quilts when they hear the word "patchwork," but it's a fun and versatile technique that can also be used to create a variety of other projects, including accessories, garments and home décor. Learn simple steps for creating patchwork masterpieces.

PATCHWORK 101

Patchwork refers to a simple process of combining fabric pieces to create a larger surface, so it's ideal for using up small scraps. The smaller pieces can be randomly combined or pieced into an organized design. Most organized patchwork designs are comprised of smaller pieced panels called blocks. When creating a quilt, the combined blocks form the quilt upper layer. The smallest fabric pieces in a block design are called patches. There are many traditional patchwork blocks that quilters have been using for decades, such as the four-patch block, log cabin block and pinwheel block (1). Even the most complicated-looking blocks begin with patches in simple shapes, such as squares and rectangles. The pieced patches are then cut, arranged and stitched into more complex patterns. If you can stitch a seam, you can piece a block!

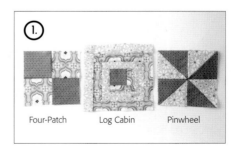

1.

Four-Patch   Log Cabin   Pinwheel

Check out Sew it All episode 304, "Patchwork Primer" at sewitalltv.com or sew.tv to learn how to stitch a pretty patchwork scarf.

It's possible to use any fabric for patchwork piecing, but most patchwork quilts are made from basic even-weave quilting cotton, which is very stable and easy to stitch. Most patchwork blocks use a ¼" seam allowance, which is wide enough to prevent raveling but narrow enough not to require trimming. Also, as opposed to garment construction, where seams are pressed open, patchwork seams are usually pressed in one direction, often toward the darker fabric. Pressing the seam in one direction distributes the bulk and protects the stitching. Careful pressing is an important part of piecing, as it flattens the block and correctly aligns the seams. Precise cutting is also important for neat patchwork, so a rotary cutting system is very handy for accurately measuring and cutting patches.

STITCH A BLOCK

Practice patchwork piecing by stitching one of the simplest designs: the four-patch block. The finished block is a 6" square.

Select two contrasting quilting cotton fabrics. Designate one as fabric A and the remaining fabric as fabric B.

Prewash the fabric before cutting to eliminate shrinkage and remove any chemicals or sizing. Wash and dry the fabric according to the fabric manufacturer's instructions.

Press the fabric along the lengthwise or crosswise grain rather than diagonally to avoid stretching or distorting the fabric.

From each fabric, cut two 3½" squares using a rotary cutting system.

Align one fabric-A square and one fabric-B square with right sides together. Stitch one edge using a ¼" seam allowance (2). Press the seam allowance toward the darker fabric (3). Repeat to stitch the remaining fabric-A and -B squares to create a second panel.

Turn the second panel so that the fabric-A and -B squares are stacked diagonally (4).

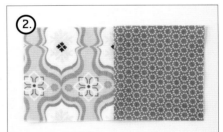

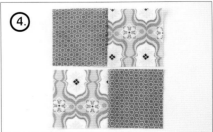

Align the panels with right sides together, carefully matching the seams; pin. Make sure the seam allowances are "nested," meaning that they are pressed in opposite directions (5). Nesting the seams reduces bulk and helps produce a neat and flat block.

Stitch the long matched edge and then unfold the block (6). Press the seam allowance downward.

If desired, stitch additional blocks to combine into a larger panel. Align the blocks with right sides together, nesting the seam allowances, and then stitch (7).

(TiP)

To make a four-patch block with a more eclectic look, cut one 3½" square each from four different fabrics.

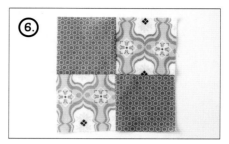

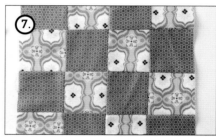

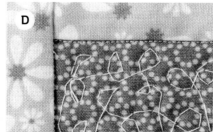

Quilting Options

When using a patchwork panel as the top of a quilted project, there are several fun quilting methods for joining the fabric and batting layers.

• **Hand Quilting (A):** Thread a needle with hand quilting thread; knot the end. Stitch a running stitch ¼" on either side of each seam.

• **Stitch in the Ditch (B):** Stitch directly over each patchwork seam.

• **Channel Quilting (C):** Stitch evenly-spaced parallel lines.

• **Free-Motion Stitching (D):** Drop the machine feed dogs, and then stitch in a random, free-form pattern. For more tips on free-motion stitching, refer to "Free-Motion Fun" in Sew it All, Volume 4.

• **Echo Quilting (E):** Stitch evenly-spaced parallel lines following or "echoing" the patch shape.

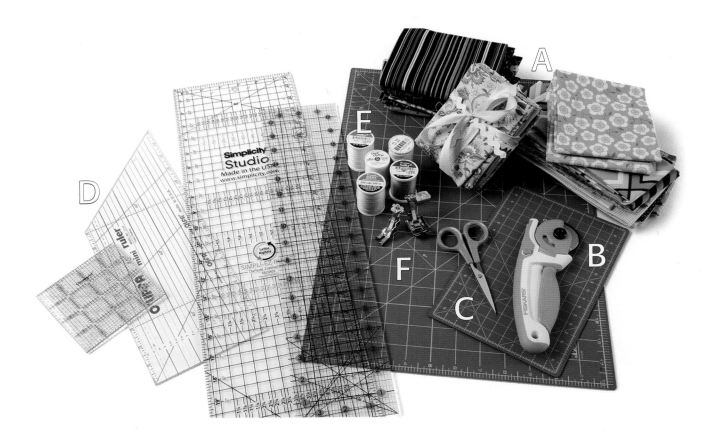

PATCHWORK TOOLS

Piece like a pro with these handy tools:

Fat Quarters (A): Patchwork quilters find these precut 18"x22" fabric rectangles especially efficient for cutting patches. Browse fabric company websites for bundles of coordinating fat quarters. Fabric companies also offer other convenient precut bundles, such as "jelly rolls," which include approximately forty 2½"x44" strips.

Rotary Cutting System (B): Rotary cutters are very effective for accurately cutting multiple fabric layers, saving you time when cutting out patches. Use a large self-healing cutting mat with marked measurements as a cutting surface.

Thread Snips or Small Scissors (C): Patchwork piecing involves many seams which result in numerous thread tails. Quickly trim away tails with small snips.

Clear Quilting Rulers (D): Quilting rulers include multiple-angle guidelines that make it easy to cut various shapes. The transparency allows you to see the layers beneath the ruler for accurate cutting.

Thread (E): When patchwork piecing, use strong, smooth thread, such as cotton quilting thread or all-purpose thread.

Specialty Feet (F): To stitch a neat ¼" seam allowance every time, use a ¼" guide foot. When quilting a patchwork project, use a ditch quilting foot to stitch in the ditch. The center guide helps to perfectly align the stitching with the seam. ❂

SOURCES
Adornit provided the Capri collection fat quarters in the taupe/gray colorway: (435) 563-1100, adornit.com.

Bernina provided the quilting feet: bernina.com.

Coats & Clark provided quilting thread: (800) 648-1479, coatsandclark.com.

Fiskars provided the Ergo Control Rotary Cutter and Detail Scissors: (866) 348- 5661, fiskars.com.

Husqvarna Viking provided the ditch quilting foot and ¼" guide foot: (800) 446-2333, husqvarnaviking.com.

Olfa provided the self-healing cutting mat and quilting rulers: (800) 962-6532, olfa.com.

Prym Consumer USA Inc. provided the Omnigrid ruler: dritz.com.

Simplicity provided the quilting ruler: (888) 588-2700 simplicity.com.

Sulky provided quilting thread: (800) 847-4115, sulky.com.

Photos courtesy of Katy Leigh Villari.

MONSTER Mash

Keep your little one clean from messy spills
by making adorable appliquéd monster bibs.

by Sara Gallegos

SUPPLIES

Supplies listed are enough to make three bibs.

Fat quarter each of 3 print cotton fabrics (See "Sources.")

¼ yard each of 2 coordinating print cotton fabrics (See "Sources.")

½ yard of coordinating print cotton fabric (See "Sources.")

½ yard of flannel

½ yard of tear-away stabilizer

Fusible web

Coordinating & matching all-purpose thread

Three 1" squares of hook-and-loop tape

PREP IT

Trace the Monster Mash patterns on pages 42-43.

From one fat quarter, cut one left and right strap and one bib for the front panel.

From the large coordinating fabric, cut one left and right strap and one bib for the back panel.

From the flannel, cut one bib.

Trace one large eye, one small eye and one mouth onto a piece of fusible web. Roughly cut out each appliqué, and then remove the upper paper-backing layers.

Fuse the appliqué pieces to the desired small coordinating-fabric wrong sides, following the manufacturer's instructions. Reference the photos at left for color combination ideas. Cut out each piece along the traced lines. Remove the remaining paper backing.

Position the appliqué pieces on the front-panel bib right side, using the photos at left for placement reference. Fuse the appliqués in place.

SEW IT

Use ¼" seam allowances unless otherwise noted.

Thread the machine with coordinating all-purpose thread and select a short, narrow blanket stitch. Position a piece of tear-away stabilizer under the front-panel bib wrong side.

Stitch each appliqué perimeter (1). Gently tear away the stabilizer beyond each appliqué perimeter.

Select a straight stitch on the machine. With right sides together, align one front-panel strap with each back-panel strap. Stitch the long curved edges, leaving the straight lower edge open for turning (2). Clip the curves, and then turn each strap right side out; press.

Position the front-panel bib right side up on a flat work surface. Pin the straps to the bib according to the pattern markings, aligning the raw edges.

Align the front- and back-panel bibs with right sides together. Position the flannel bib right side up over the back-panel bib; pin.

Stitch the bib perimeter, leaving a 2" opening along one edge for turning. Clip the curves, and then turn the bib right side out; press. Fold the opening edges ¼" toward the wrong side; press. Topstitch the bib perimeter, closing the opening with the stitches.

Position one hook-tape square along the front right-strap upper edge; edgestitch the square perimeter using matching all-purpose thread. Repeat to stitch the loop-tape square to the back left-strap upper edge.

Repeat to stitch two additional bibs using different fabrics. ✪

SOURCES

Baby Lock provided the tear-away stabilizer: babylock.com.

Cloud9 Fabrics provided the Monsterz fabric collection: (908) 403-2461, cloud9fabrics.com.

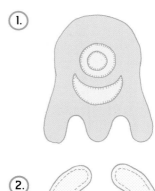

(TiP)
When pivoting fabric, raise the presser foot and keep the needle in the fabric to prevent misaligned stitches.

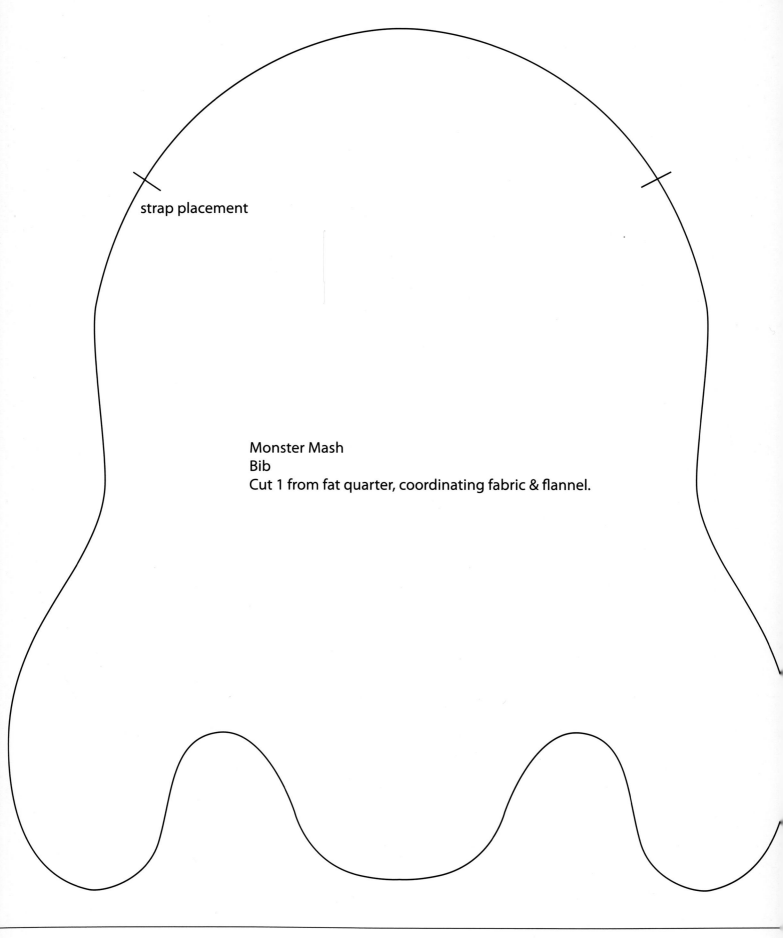

strap placement

Monster Mash
Bib
Cut 1 from fat quarter, coordinating fabric & flannel.

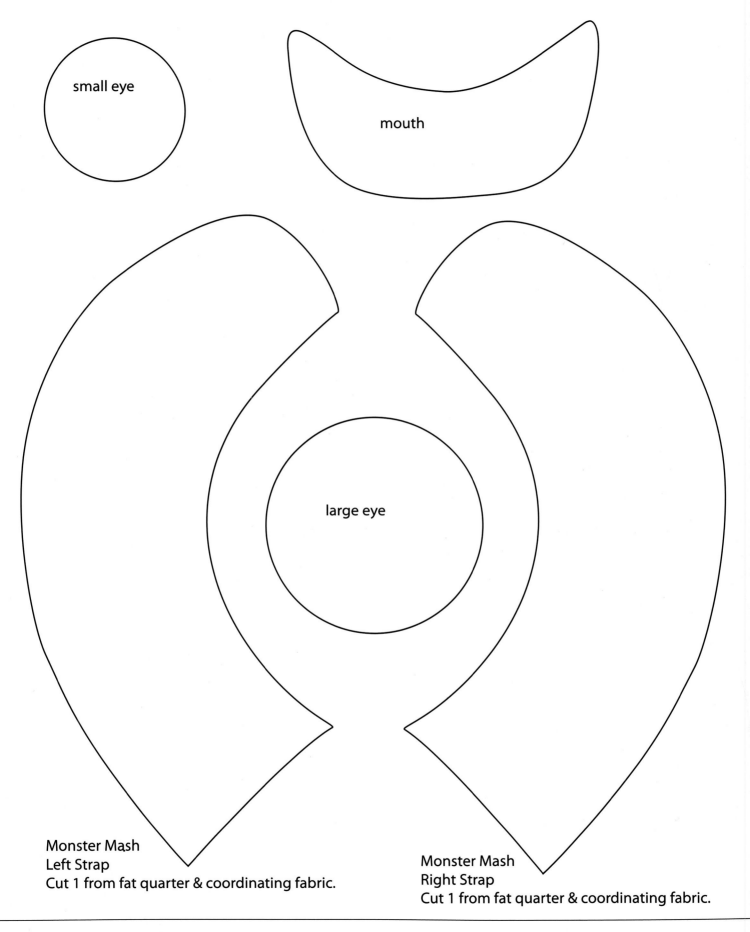

small eye

mouth

large eye

Monster Mash
Left Strap
Cut 1 from fat quarter & coordinating fabric.

Monster Mash
Right Strap
Cut 1 from fat quarter & coordinating fabric.

APPLIQUÉ AWAY

by Kim Saba

Traditional appliqué is the process of stitching one shaped fabric piece to another. The technique is simple and creative and one that anyone can master. Best of all, it's easily adaptable to many fun projects.

Layer Upon Layer

Take appliqué to another level by layering pieces to create texture and dimension.

- Select an appliqué design that lends itself to layering design details to create distinct attributes, such as faces or flowers (shown left).

- Layer different appliqués to create a dimensional scene. For example, create a garden scene with grass in the background, flowers layered over the grass and a butterfly layered over the flowers.

- Create shadows by selecting two or three varying shades of the same fabric color. Layer the darker shades in the background and lighter shades in the foreground.

Design School

Use ready-made appliqué designs. Download free appliqué designs from websites, such as freeapplique.com or weefolkart.com. Or purchase appliqué design books dedicated to certain categories, such as animals, flowers and letters.

Create your own appliqué designs. Select basic shapes with smooth outlines and minimal details, such as hearts, stars or circles. More intricate designs, such as animals and flowers, should have a distinct but smooth outline without a lot of sharp corners or small curves (1). Use your own drawings, children's coloring book images, cookie cutters or clip art for appliqué designs.

Target specific motifs from print fabric to use as appliqué pieces (this technique is called "fussy cutting"). Adhere a piece of fusible web to the selected motif on the fabric wrong side, following the manufacturer's instructions. Fussy cut the appliqué piece slightly beyond the motif outline (2).

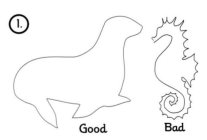

Good Bad

Use a die template and die-cutting machine to easily create precise appliqué pieces in an array of fun shapes. Follow the manufacturer's instructions to cut the desired appliqué shapes from the fabric (3).

(TiP)

Hand embroidery is great for
attaching or embellishing appliqués!

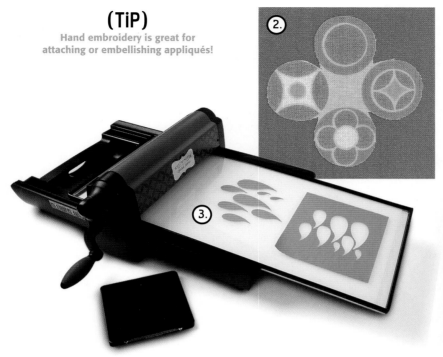

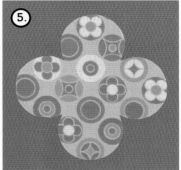

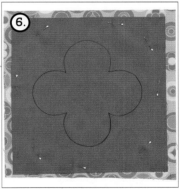

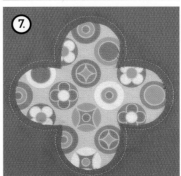

Basic Training

After selecting a design, draw, trace
or print it out. Place a piece of double-
sided fusible web over the design right
side with the paper backing right side
up. Trace the design using a pen, pencil
or marker. Roughly cut out the appliqué
approximately ½″ to 1″ beyond the design
outline (4).

Fuse the appliqué to the chosen fabric
wrong side with the paper backing right
side up. Carefully cut out the design using
small sharp scissors.

Remove the paper backing and fuse
the appliqué to the desired fabric or
project right side (5).

Stitch the appliqué perimeter using
one of the stitching options listed in
"Which Stitch" on page 46.

Put it in Reverse

Reverse appliqué is the opposite of basic
appliqué: One layer of fabric is cut away to
expose a second fabric underneath. Don't
be nervous; it's still a simple technique
that just requires some careful cutting.

After selecting a design, draw, trace
or print it out. Trace the design onto
the upper fabric layer right side, using a
removable fabric marker or chalk.

Cut a piece of the lower fabric 3″
to 4″ larger than the appliqué design
perimeter. Position the upper fabric layer
wrong side over the lower fabric layer
right side, making sure that the appliqué
design is centered over the lower fabric
layer; pin 1″ to 2″ beyond the design
perimeter (6).

Stitch along the design line through
both fabric layers using one of the
stitching options listed in "Which Stitch"
on page 46.

Using appliqué scissors, cut away
the upper fabric ⅛″ to ¼″ inside the
stitching line. Be very careful not to cut
through the lower fabric layer (7). ✪

WHICH STITCH?

Finish your fantastic appliqué by choosing from a variety of stitch options. Thread the machine with coordinating or contrasting thread and always center the stitching along the appliqué raw edge unless otherwise noted.

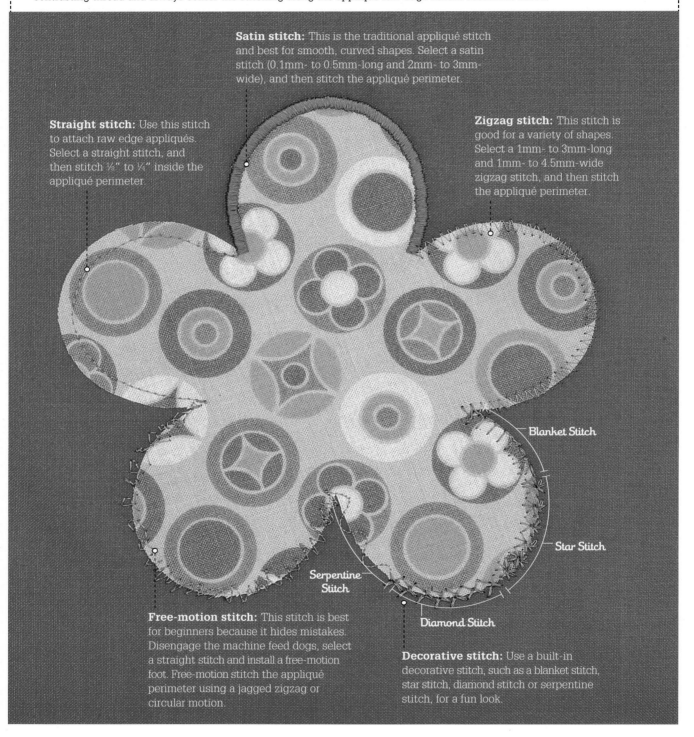

Satin stitch: This is the traditional appliqué stitch and best for smooth, curved shapes. Select a satin stitch (0.1mm- to 0.5mm-long and 2mm- to 3mm-wide), and then stitch the appliqué perimeter.

Straight stitch: Use this stitch to attach raw edge appliqués. Select a straight stitch, and then stitch ⅛" to ¼" inside the appliqué perimeter.

Zigzag stitch: This stitch is good for a variety of shapes. Select a 1mm- to 3mm-long and 1mm- to 4.5mm-wide zigzag stitch, and then stitch the appliqué perimeter.

Blanket Stitch

Star Stitch

Serpentine Stitch

Diamond Stitch

Free-motion stitch: This stitch is best for beginners because it hides mistakes. Disengage the machine feed dogs, select a straight stitch and install a free-motion foot. Free-motion stitch the appliqué perimeter using a jagged zigzag or circular motion.

Decorative stitch: Use a built-in decorative stitch, such as a blanket stitch, star stitch, diamond stitch or serpentine stitch, for a fun look.

AWESOME APPLIQUÉ

These helpful tools make appliqué even easier:

1. Appliqué pins are the old school way of attaching an appliqué piece to fabric without using fusible web. Appliqué pins are short (usually ¾"-long) so they're easy to maneuver when stitching.

2. Thread adds excitement to basic appliqués. Experiment with metallic, variegated, glow-in-the-dark or neon thread to achieve a variety of fun looks.

3. Mini irons are great for pressing small appliqués or hard to reach areas. Pair a small iron with a table top ironing board next to your sewing machine for quick pressing, especially when working with multiple appliqué layers.

4. A PTFE pressing sheet is the product you'll never believe you lived without. It protects your iron and appliqué from fusible gunk when pressing, leaving clean and precise appliqués.

5. Temporary spray adhesive is great if you don't have fusible web on hand. Spray the adhesive onto the appliqué wrong side and finger-press it to the fabric right side. If you don't like the placement, simply reposition the appliqué before stitching.

6. Fusible web is your best friend when creating appliqués. It comes in a variety of types, including double-sided sheets and tape, water-soluble and silicone transfer. If you have an intricate design or just dislike tracing, some fusible web types can be used in inkjet printers, which will print the desired design directly onto the fusible web paper backing.

7. Scissors are an absolute must-have for flawless appliqué. Invest in a small sharp pair for cutting out and trimming intricate appliqués, a blunt curved pair for iron-on appliqués and duckbill/pelican appliqué scissors for large reverse appliqués.

SOURCES

Baby Lock provided the Ellisimo sewing and embroidery machine used to create the featured samples: babylock.com.

C&T Publishing provided the silicone release paper and wash-away appliqué sheets: (800) 284-1114, ctpub.com.

Clover Needlecraft provided the appliqué pins, mini iron and patchwork scissors: (800) 233-1703, clover-usa.com.

Coats & Clark provided the glow-in-the-dark and neon thread: (800) 648-1479, coatsandclark.com.

Ellison provided the Sizzix Big Shot Pro die-cutting machine by Westminster Fibers and Petals, Leaves, Tear Drop 656669 Bigz Die: (877) 355-4766, sizzix.com.

Havel's provided the curved-end, double curved blunt tip pelican and embroidery scissors: (800) 638-4770, havelssewing.com.

Nancy's Notions provided the appliqué pins, lift and cut scissors, micro-serrated scissors and PTFE pressing sheet: (800) 833-0690, nancysnotions.com.

Sulky of America provided the metallic and variegated thread and temporary spray adhesive: (800) 874-4115, sulky.com.

Therm O Web provided the HeatnBond Lite fusible web tape: (800) 323-0799, thermowebonline.com.

The Warm Company provided Steam-A-Seam fusible web, Steam-A-Seam 2 double-stick fusible web and Steam-A-Seam 2 double-stick fusible web tape: (425) 248-2424, warmcompany.com.

TIES FOR TOTS

Quickly stitch a bowtie for the little man in your life to wear to weddings, church or other special events.

by Kim Saba

SUPPLIES

Supplies listed are enough to make one size 12m to 3T bowtie.

Fat quarter of print cotton fabric (See "Source.")

All-purpose thread

½"x1" length of hook-and-loop tape

Hand sewing needle

CUT IT

From the print cotton, cut one 4½" square for the lower bow, one 4"x4½" rectangle for the upper bow and one 1¾"x2¼" rectangle for the tie.

Measure the child's neck circumference; add ½", and then record. From the print cotton, cut one strip measuring 1½"x the recorded measurement for the neck strap.

SEW IT

Use ¼" seam allowances.

Fold the upper and lower bows, tie and neck strap in half lengthwise with right sides together; press. Designate each upper and lower bow folded edge as the upper edge.

Stitch the upper and lower bow sides and lower edge, leaving a centered ¾"-long opening along the lower edge for turning. Clip the lower-edge corners. Turn the upper and lower bows right side out through the opening; press.

Center the upper bow over the lower bow; pin. Thread a hand sewing needle with a length of thread; knot the end. Fold the layers in half lengthwise with the upper bow together. Fold each long edge toward the lower layer, aligning the edges with the lengthwise center fold. Hand stitch the bow widthwise center to secure (1).

Stitch the tie long edge and one short edge with right sides together. Turn the tie right side out; press.

Wrap the tie around the bow widthwise center, lapping the finished edge ⅛" over the raw edge; pin. Whipstitch the tie to secure, making sure to not catch the bow in the stitching.

Stitch the neck strap long edge and one short edge with right sides together. Turn the strap right side out; press. Designate a strap right and wrong side. Thread one strap short edge through the tie, centering the strap with the strap right side facing the bowtie.

Fold the strap raw short edge ¼" toward the right side; press. Center the loop tape over the strap raw short edge on the right side; edge-stitch the perimeter.

Center the hook tape over the opposite-strap short edge on the wrong side; edgestitch the perimeter (2). ✪

SOURCE

Fat Quarter Shop provided the Lollipop Sweater Check and Pencil Sweater Check fabric from the *Little Apples* collection by Aneela Hoey for Moda Fabrics: (866) 826-2069, fatquartershop.com.

1.

2.

Pin Me!

Instead of using a neck strap, center a pin back on the bow wrong side; hand stitch.

DOUBLE DUTY DUVET

by Carol Zentgraf

Give a bedroom a fresh update with a duvet cover. Piece panels on one side and add a contrasting print on the reverse for two entirely different décor options.

SUPPLIES

Supplies listed are enough to make one 67"x88" duvet cover.

5½ yards each of two coordinating 44"-wide fabrics for the front and back (See "Sources.")

2¾ yards of coordinating 44"-wide fabric for the borders (See "Sources.")

1 yard of ½"-wide soft hook-and-loop tape

½"-wide double-sided fusible web (See "Sources.")

Coordinating all-purpose thread (See "Sources.")

CUT IT

Designate one coordinating fabric as the front and one as the back.

From the front fabric, cut one 40"x76" rectangle for the center, two 11½"x76" strips for the outer side panels, one 9½"x69" strip for the outer lower panel and two 3"x69" strips for the front and back upper edge.

From the back fabric, cut one 44"x88" rectangle and one 44"x98" rectangle.

From the border fabric, cut two 5"x76" strips for the sides, one 5"x49" strip for the lower edge and two 5"x11½" rectangles for the outer border ends.

SEW IT

Use ½" seam allowances and refer to the diagram above for the layout.

With right sides together, align one side-border strip with each center-panel long edge; stitch. Press the seams toward the borders.

With right sides together, align the lower border strip with the center and side-border lower edge; stitch. Press the seam toward the center.

With right sides together, align one outer-border long edge with each outer-side short edge; stitch. Press the seam toward the border.

With the outer border at the upper edge, align the outer side panel and inner panel long edges, stitch. Press the seams toward the outer border.

With right sides together, align the outer lower panel with the pieced panel lower edge; stitch. Press the seam toward the center.

With wrong sides together, fold the front upper-edge fabric strip in half lengthwise; press. Align the strip raw edges with the front-panel upper edge right side; stitch. Press the seam allowance toward the panel, and then topstitch.

Cut the selvages off both back-fabric panel pieces.

Along the larger back-panel long edge, apply fusible web to the right side following the manufacturer's instructions. Don't remove the paper backing. Using the tape as a guide, fold the edge ½" toward the wrong side; press (1).

Place the remaining back panel right side up on a large flat pressing surface. Remove the paper backing from the fusible web, and then overlap the panel long edges, adjusting until the motifs are perfectly matched; fuse (2).

On the fused-panels wrong side, stitch along the top-panel foldline through all layers. Trim the panel to 69"x88".

Fold the remaining upper-edge fabric strip in half lengthwise with wrong sides together; press. Align the strip raw edges with one back-panel short edge; stitch. Press the seam allowance toward the back panel; topstitch.

FINISH IT

With right sides together, stitch the front and back together along the side and lower edges. Turn right side out, and then press.

Cut the hook-and-loop tape into four equal sections. Evenly space the tape pieces along the border; stitch each hook-and-loop tape piece perimeter. ✪

SOURCES

Coats & Clark provided the Dual Duty sewing thread: coatsandclark.com.

Warm Company provided the fusible web: warmcompany.com.

Westminster Fibers provided the Amy Butler Cameo fabric collection: www.westminsterfibers.com.

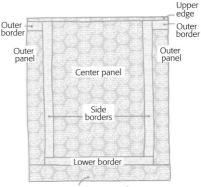

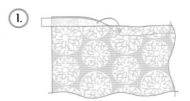

(TiP) Turn the cover to the opposite side for a quick décor switch.

TUFT STUFF

by Beth Bradley

Round out your décor with a reversible circular pillow that you can complete in an afternoon.

SUPPLIES

Supplies listed are enough to make one 14"-diameter pillow.

½ yard each of two coordinating home-décor fabrics (A & B; see "Sources")

All-purpose thread

Polyester fiberfill or 14"-diameter round pillow form (See "Sources.")

Two 1¼"-diameter cover button kits

Straight upholstery needle

CUT IT

Trace the Tuft Stuff pattern on page 53. From fabrics A and B, cut eight wedges each.

SEW IT

Use ¼" seam allowances.

Align two fabric-A wedges with right sides together. Stitch one long edge; press open the seam.

With right sides together, align one fabric-A wedge long edge with the pieced-panel right edge; stitch (1). Press open the seam. Repeat to construct a four-wedge half-circle panel, and then stitch the remaining fabric-A wedges into a second four-wedge panel.

With right sides together, align the two half-circle panels; pin. Stitch the long straight edge (2). Press open the seam.

Repeat to construct the fabric-B wedges into a circular panel.

With right sides together, align the two circular panels, matching the seams; pin. Stitch the panel circumference, leaving a 5" opening for turning. Press open the seam along the ironing board edge or using a tailor's ham.

Turn the cover right side out through the opening. Stuff the pillow firmly with fiberfill or insert the pillow form. Slipstitch the opening closed.

FINISH IT

Follow the cover button kit instructions to cover one button each with fabric-A and fabric-B scraps.

Thread a straight upholstery needle with a double thread strand; knot the ends. Insert the needle at the fabric-A center, and bring it up through the fabric-B center. Position the fabric-A button on the pillow fabric-B center, and then hand stitch it in place through all layers to tuft the pillow. Repeat to stitch the fabric-B button to the pillow fabric-A center. ✪

SOURCES

Fairfield provided the Soft Touch Poly-Fil Supreme Fiberfill: (800) 980-8000, fairfieldworld.com.

Harmony Art Fabrics provided the brown and aqua organic cotton twill fabrics: harmonyart.com.

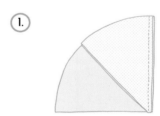

①

②

Stitch.

(TiP)

For a funky effect, piece each pillow panel using a variety of scraps from your fabric stash.

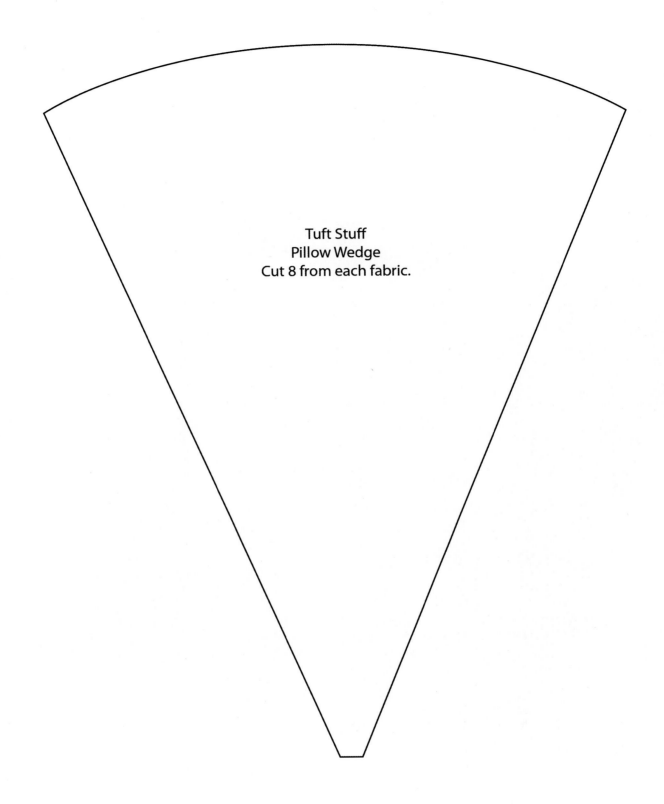

Tuft Stuff
Pillow Wedge
Cut 8 from each fabric.

ROSY OUTLOOK

Create a stunning pillow full of roses using soft luxurious wool.

by Kate Van Fleet

✳ Refer to, "Do the Ruffle" on page 56 for more ruffle-making tips.

SUPPLIES

1⅝ yards of 52"-wide 100% wool (See "Source.")

Matching all-purpose thread

Dental floss or string

Tailor's chalk

Clear tape

Hand sewing needle

16"-square pillow form

CUT IT

From the wool, cut two 16½" squares for the pillow and 25 strips measuring 3"x26" for the roses.

SEW IT

Using tailor's chalk, freehand draw scallops along one long edge of each strip; cut along the scallop edge.

Position a length of dental floss or string along one strip straight long edge, extending the floss at least 3" beyond each strip end. Set the machine for a 4mm- to 5mm-wide zigzag stitch. Zigzag stitch over the floss (1). Carefully pull each floss end independently, gathering the strip ends toward the center until the strip is half of the original length. Evenly distribute the gathers.

Roll one strip into a rose shape, hand stitching the straight long edges to each other as you roll. Loosely roll the strip rose to create a rose with a 5"-diameter base. Repeat to create 24 additional roses.

With right sides together, stitch the pillow squares along the perimeter, using a ¼" seam allowance and leaving a 6" opening along one edge. Designate the opening edge as the lower edge. Insert the pillow form through the opening. Slipstitch the opening closed.

Using clear tape, mark a 25-square grid on the pillow front (2). Each square should measure approximately 4".

Position one rose wrong side down over the pillow-front right side, centering the

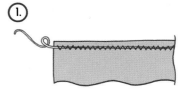

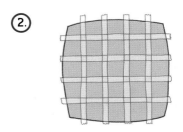

rose base inside one square grid. Hand stitch the rose base to the pillow front. Continue to stitch one rose to each square. Carefully remove the tape grid. ✛

SOURCE
Weeks Dye Works provided the Merlot hand over-dyed wool: (877) 683-7393, weeksdyeworks.com.

DO THE RUFFLE

Ruffles add flounce and fun to any project or garment.
Learn the ins and outs for perfect ruffles every time.

by Kim Saba

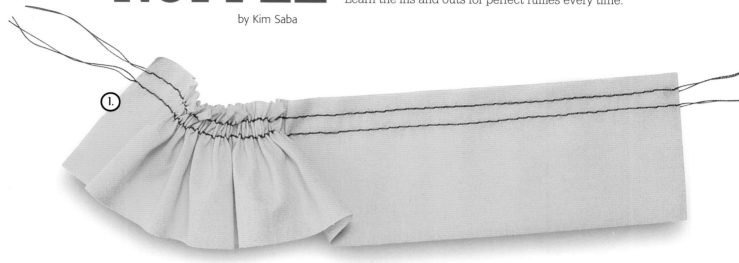

GATHERS VS. RUFFLES

It's easy to confuse gathers and ruffles because they're similar in technique but different in style.

Gathers add fullness to a garment with one or two rows of stitching that compress the fabric into soft folds. Gathers usually fit a predetermined shorter length, such as a gathered skirt waistline attached to a bodice.

Ruffles are strips of tightly-gathered

fabric that are usually attached to a project edge, such as a skirt hem.

GATHER 'ROUND

Discover simple ways to easily create gathers for ravishing ruffles.

BASTED AWAY

Select a 4mm- to 5mm-long basting stitch. Stitch ½" from the fabric raw edge, leaving long thread tails at the stitching beginning and end. Stitch another basting stitch row ¼" from the raw edge, leaving long thread tails at the stitching beginning and end. Gently pull the bobbin tails to gather the fabric to the desired length (1); evenly distribute the gathers. For heavyweight fabrics, use heavyweight thread in the bobbin for extra strength while gathering.

STRING THING

Select a 3mm- to 3.5mm-long zigzag stitch. Position a string or cord length 4" longer than the fabric piece just inside the seamline along the seam allowance. Tack

down one cord end. Center the presser foot over the string, and then zigzag stitch over the string or cord. Gently pull the string or cord to gather the fabric to the desired length, making sure not to pull the opposite end through the stitching (2); evenly distribute the gathers along the cord. Remove the cord after attaching to the fabric or garment. This method works best for heavyweight fabrics, such as home-décor fabrics.

A LENGTHY MATTER

To determine the fabric strip length needed to create a ruffle, double or triple the desired finished length. For example, if a 20"-long ruffle is needed, cut a 40"- or 60"-long fabric strip. The longer the fabric length, the tighter the gathers. Heavyweight fabric requires a shorter fabric length and a lightweight fabric requires a longer fabric length to create the same amount of gathers. Piece together strips as needed to create the desired length.

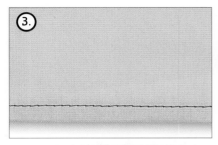

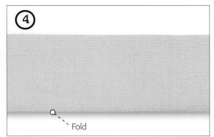

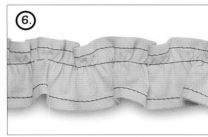

Fold

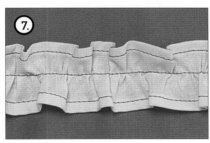

STRAIGHT & NARROW

Straight ruffles are fabric strips cut on the crosswise or bias grain and may have one or two fabric layers.

A single-layer ruffle is one fabric layer with a rolled hem finish on one long edge (3). Tightly gather the opposite long edge to create a ruffle.

A self-faced ruffle is a fabric strip folded in half lengthwise with wrong sides together. Use this type of ruffle when both ruffle sides are visible or with lightweight fabrics to add more stability and structure (4). Tightly gather the long raw edge through both fabric layers to create a ruffle.

RUFF 'EM UP

Learn three methods to construct a straight single-layer or self-faced ruffle.

To create a plain ruffle, finish one long edge and attach the opposite long edge to a fabric or garment raw edge (5).

To create a ruffle with a heading, finish both long edges and gather ⅓ to ¼ the strip width from one finished edge (6).

To create a double ruffle, finish both long edges and gather the strip center. Pin the ruffle to a project or garment and topstitch along the ruffle center (7). ✤

SOURCES

Baby Lock provided the gathering feet:
(800) 422-2952, babylock.com.

Brother provided the ruffle foot/attachment:
(877) 276-8437, brother-usa.com.

IN CIRCLES

Circular ruffles, also called "flounces," are cut in a circle shape from one fabric layer. Rather than being gathered, a small circle is cut out from the center of a large circle to create fullness. The circle short edge lays flat, creating ruffles on the long outer edge (A). Circular ruffles are best for necklines and lightweight sheer fabric.

To draft a circular ruffle pattern, measure the project edge length where the ruffle will be attached; record. On a piece of pattern paper, draw a circle with a circumference according to the recorded measurement. Designate the circle as the inner edge.

Draw a circle the desired ruffle width beyond the small circle. Designate the circle as the outer edge. Add the desired seam allowances to the large circle outer and inner edges.

Draw a straight line from the large circle outer edge to the inner edge, creating the ruffle cutting line (B).

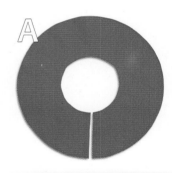

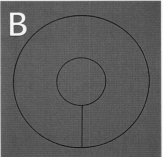

SITTING PRETTY

by Kate Van Fleet

Jazz up a basic folding chair with a comfy padded cushion and matching backrest slipcover. Heavyweight home-dec fabric provides durability, and fusible fleece simplifies the sewing process.

(TiP)

Experiment with the chair cushion and slipcover look by tying the ties different ways.

SUPPLIES

Supplies listed are enough to make one cushion and one slipcover to fit a standard folding chair.

Approximately 1 yard of 55"-wide heavyweight home-dec fabric or canvas duck (amount determined by chair measurements)

Approximately 1½ yards of fusible fleece (amount determined by chair measurements)

Matching heavyweight thread

MEASURE IT

Measure the backrest width circumference. Divide the measurement by two and add seam allowances and ease; record. Depending on the backrest depth, more or less ease may be needed. Measure the depth and adjust the final measurement to account for more or less ease. The featured backrest is 1" deep and uses ½" seam allowances, so an additional 2" was added to the width measurement.

Measure the desired backrest slipcover length. For the featured slipcover, the lower edges extend 8" beyond the backrest lower edge. Measure from the desired slipcover lower edge to the backrest upper edge. Add 3" to the length measurement; record.

Measure the chair seat length and width; add 2" to each measurement; record.

CUT IT

Cut two slipcovers each from the fabric and fleece, according to the recorded measurements. Trim ½" away from each fleece edge.

Cut two cushions each from the fabric and fleece, according to the recorded measurements. Trim ½" away from each fleece edge.

From the leftover fabric, cut eight 1½"x8" strips for the ties.

SEW IT

Use ½" seam allowances unless otherwise noted.

Fold one end of each tie ¼" to the wrong side; press. Fold each tie in half lengthwise with wrong sides together; press, and then unfold. Fold each long raw edge ¼" to the wrong side; press. Refold each strip along the center foldline. Stitch close to the long-edge fold and along the folded end; set aside each strip.

Center each fleece piece on each corresponding fabric wrong side; fuse, following the manufacturer's instructions.

Position two tie raw ends together as one unit on one cushion right side along one corner; pin. Repeat to pin two additional ties along the opposite cushion corner.

Position the remaining slipcover over the pinned cushion with right sides together; pin the perimeter, making sure the ties are inside the cushion "sandwich."

Stitch the cushion perimeter, leaving a 6" opening along one edge for turning. Turn the cushion right side out through the opening. Press the opening edges ½" to the wrong side; slipstitch the opening closed.

With right sides together, stitch the slipcover sides and upper edge. Serge- or zigzag-finish the lower edge. Fold the lower edge 1" to the wrong side; press. Insert two strip raw ends into the hem fold at one side seam; pin. Insert the remaining strip raw ends into the hem fold at the opposite side seam; pin. Stitch ¾" from the lower-edge fold, securing the ties with the stitching. Turn the slipcover right side out.

Slip the slipcover around the backrest; tie the ties into a bow around each back chair leg. Position the cushion on the chair seat with the ties facing the seat back. Tie the ties into a bow around each back chair leg. ✪

SOURCE
Fabric.com provided the fusible fleece: (888) 455-2940, fabric.com.

LOG CABIN FEVER

by Beth Bradley

Stitch unique place mats to decorate your dining table using a modified log cabin piecing technique.

SUPPLIES

Supplies listed are enough to make two 13½"x18" place mats.

½ yard each of linen or linen-blend fabric, fusible fleece & print cotton fabric (A; see "Source")

1 fat quarter each of 4 coordinating print cotton fabrics (B, C, D & E; see "Source")

Thread: coordinating all-purpose & embroidery floss or Perle cotton

Needles: hand sewing & embroidery

Safety pins (optional)

CUT IT

From the linen, cut two 5½"x6½" rectangles, two 2"x11½" strips and enough strips to equal 128" including ¼" seam allowances.

From fabric A, cut two 13½"x18" rectangles, two 2½"x8½" strips and two 1¾"x11¾" strips.

From fabric B, cut two 2½"x6½" strips and two 3"x11¾" strips.

From fabric C, cut two 2"x7" strips and two 2"x16½" strips.

From fabric D, cut two 2"x9½" strips and two 2½"x9" strips.

From fabric E, cut two 2½"x11" strips and two 2½"x13" strips.

From the fusible fleece, cut two 13½"x18" rectangles.

SEW IT

Use ¼" seam allowances.

Designate one linen-rectangle long edge as the upper edge. With right sides together, align one short fabric-B strip long edge with the linen rectangle upper edge; stitch. Press the seam toward the linen. With right sides together, align one short fabric-C strip long edge with the pieced-panel right long edge; stitch. Press the seam toward the fabric-C strip (1). Evenly trim the strip ends if needed.

With right sides together, align one short fabric-A strip long edge with the panel lower long edge; stitch. Press the seam toward the fabric-A strip. With right sides together, align one wide fabric-D strip long edge with the panel left edge; stitch. With right sides together, align one narrow fabric-D strip with the panel right edge; stitch (2). Evenly trim the strip ends if needed, and press the seams toward the fabric-D strips.

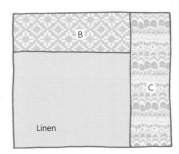

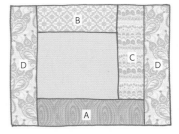

(TiP)

Create place mats with matching log cabin layouts, or mix and match the fabric strip placements for an eclectic effect.

(3.)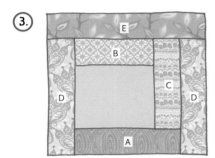

(4.)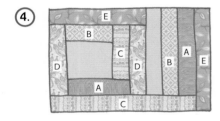

(5.)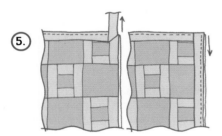

(6.)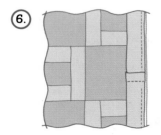

With right sides together, align one short fabric-E strip long edge with the panel upper long edge; stitch. Press the seam toward the fabric-E strip (3).

Continue piecing the remaining fabric strips with right sides together to construct a finished upper panel according to the diagram; press (4). Repeat to construct the second upper panel.

Fuse one fleece rectangle to each upper-panel wrong side following the manufacturer's instructions. Align one upper panel with each fabric-A rectangle with right sides together. Baste the layers together using safety pins or a long running stitch.

Thread the embroidery needle with embroidery floss or Perle cotton; knot the end. Hand stitch a ⅜"-long running stitch ¼" within each linen rectangle perimeter. Repeat to hand stitch several other random strip perimeters as desired.

Remove the safety pins or basting stitches.

FINISH IT

With right sides together, piece the binding strip short edges to create two 64"-long continuous strips.

Fold one binding short end ½" toward the fabric wrong side. Fold the binding in half lengthwise with wrong sides together.

Position the binding folded short end along one place-mat long edge with right sides together and raw edges aligned. Begin stitching through all layers 2" from the folded short end.

At each corner, raise the needle, rotate the place mat 90°, and then fold the binding up and back down over itself to form a mitered corner. Lower the needle and continue stitching (5).

End the stitching 1" before the binding beginning. Trim the binding end to fit inside the beginning fold. Insert the raw end into the beginning fold (6). Continue stitching to finish attaching the binding.

Fold the binding toward the place mat back, enclosing the raw edges and covering the machine stitching. Slipstitch the binding fold to the place mat back, mitering each corner.

Repeat to bind the remaining place mat. ✪

SOURCE

Fabric.com provided the Moda Serenade fabric collection: (888) 455-2940, fabric.com.

MEET THE MACHINE

Familiarize yourself with sewing lingo before you start machine shopping. Here's a crash course on the basic sewing machine parts.

Spool Holder (A): This horizontal or vertical pin holds the thread spool. Some machines have more than one spool holder to allow for double-needle or decorative stitching.

Bobbin (B): A bobbin is a small plastic or metal thread spool that lives under the sewing machine needle plate. As you sew a seam, thread from the bobbin is picked up by the thread in the needle to form a strong 2-thread stitch, also called a straight stitch or lockstitch.

Bobbin Winder (C): The bobbin winder is a small pin that winds thread from the spool onto the bobbin. The bobbin winder is usually located on the top or front of the machine and is operated by the foot pedal or a designated button on the machine face.

Take-Up Lever (D): The upper thread flows through this little lever to ensure smooth sewing and even tension.

Stitch Width & Length Controls (E): These buttons or dials control the stitch length and width (the numbers refer to millimeters). For a straight stitch, you only need to worry about the length. For a decorative or zigzag stitch, you can fiddle with the width as well.

Hand Wheel (F): The hand wheel allows you to slowly operate the machine by hand for extra control. As you turn it, you'll see the needle and take-up lever bob up and down.

Tension Control (G): This dial or button controls the amount of pressure applied to the thread to form an even stitch. When the tension is adjusted properly for a basic straight stitch, the "lock" (the knot that's formed between the upper and lower thread) is hidden between the fabric layers, forming a strong seam.

Stitch Selection Control (H): In addition to the basic straight stitch, most sewing machines have a variety of functional and decorative stitches. Usually more advanced machines have more built-in stitches. Some machines have thousands of stitches to choose from!

Light (I): This small but mighty light bulb illuminates the sewing area to help you see your handiwork clearly and prevent eye fatigue.

Reverse Control (J): While most of the time you'll be sewing forward, it's also important to be able to sew backward. When you reach the end of a seam, you can secure the stitching line by pressing the reverse button or lever and stitching backward for a few stitches, also called backstitching.

Presser Foot (K): The presser foot applies downward pressure as you sew to help guide the fabric. Its up-and-down motion is controlled by a little lever that's usually located on the back or side of the machine. When you're sewing, the presser foot should always be in the "down" position. Every sewing machine comes with a standard presser foot that works for most basic sewing tasks. However, most machines also come with a few additional presser feet designed especially for other tasks, such as inserting a zipper or stitching a buttonhole. Your sewing machine dealer or manufacturer will also carry many other useful specialty feet to purchase separately.

Needle (L): The needle is threaded from the upper thread spool. It pierces the fabric, picking up thread from the bobbin to form a stitch. Needles get dull after lots of sewing, so they need to be periodically replaced. Different needles are designed for different fabrics, but a universal needle will work for most basic sewing. Some machines also come with a handy needle-threading mechanism.

Thread Cutter (M): Mechanical machines often have a small protected blade that's located on the back or side of the machine near the needle. After sewing a seam, cut the thread on the blade. Some electronic machines have a nifty push-button control that automatically cuts the thread for you.

Throat Plate & Feed Dogs (N): The throat plate is the removable metal plate that protects the bobbin and sewing machine insides. It usually has embossed lines or seam guides marked with various measurements. Beneath the throat plate, you'll find the feed dogs (no, we're not talking about Fido or his dinner). These small metal bars move back and forth, pulling or "feeding" the fabric under the presser foot as you sew.

Foot Pedal: This pedal works just like the gas pedal in your car. It controls the machine's motor, so the harder you press, the faster it goes. It rests on the floor and is attached to the machine by a cord. Some new electronic machines can also operate with the push of a button. ✪

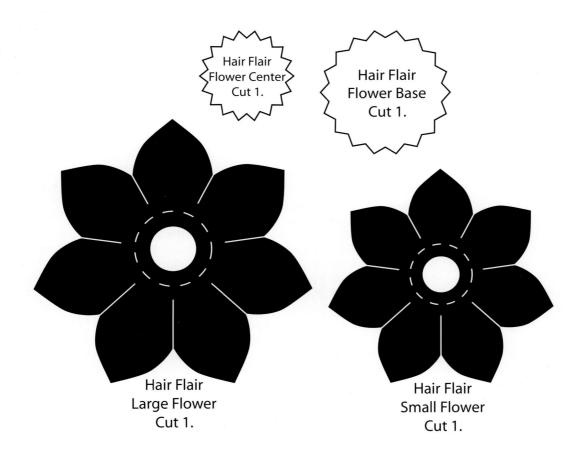

Hair Flair Flower Center Cut 1.

Hair Flair Flower Base Cut 1.

Hair Flair Large Flower Cut 1.

Hair Flair Small Flower Cut 1.